T0219606

Getting Started with Enterprise Architecture

A Practical and Pragmatic Approach to Learning the Basics of Enterprise Architecture

Eric Jager

Foreword by Whynde Kuehn

Apress®

Getting Started with Enterprise Architecture: A Practical and Pragmatic Approach to Learning the Basics of Enterprise Architecture

Eric Jager
Almere, Flevoland, The Netherlands

ISBN-13 (pbk): 978-1-4842-9857-2   ISBN-13 (electronic): 978-1-4842-9858-9
https://doi.org/10.1007/978-1-4842-9858-9

Managing Director, Apress Media LLC: Welmoed Spahr
Acquisitions Editor: Aditee Mirashi
Development Editor: James Markham
Editorial Assistant: Jessica Vakili

Cover designed by eStudioCalamar

Cover image designed by Eric Jager

Distributed to the book trade worldwide by Springer Science+Business Media New York, 1 New York Plaza, Suite 4600, New York, NY 10004-1562, USA. Phone 1-800-SPRINGER, fax (201) 348-4505, e-mail orders-ny@springer-sbm.com, or visit www.springeronline.com. Apress Media, LLC is a California LLC and the sole member (owner) is Springer Science + Business Media Finance Inc (SSBM Finance Inc). SSBM Finance Inc is a **Delaware** corporation.

For information on translations, please e-mail booktranslations@springernature.com; for reprint, paperback, or audio rights, please e-mail bookpermissions@springernature.com.

Apress titles may be purchased in bulk for academic, corporate, or promotional use. eBook versions and licenses are also available for most titles. For more information, reference our Print and eBook Bulk Sales web page at http://www.apress.com/bulk-sales.

Any source code or other supplementary material referenced by the author in this book is available to readers on GitHub. For more detailed information, please visit https://www.apress.com/gp/services/source-code.

Paper in this product is recyclable

Table of Contents

About the Author

 **Eric Jager** is a *Certified Master Architect* in the field of Enterprise Architecture. He is also a certified TOGAF Enterprise Architecture Practitioner, Certified Business Architect, and ArchiMate Practitioner. He is familiar with various architecture methodologies including, for example, the TOGAF Standard and the Zachman Framework.

The inspiration for this book came from Eric's work experience in organizations with regulatory functions in both the financial and healthcare industries, commercial service providers, and several hospitals. There, he noticed that organizations continued to struggle with properly implementing architectural thinking and working with architecture. Eric set out to create an easy-to-understand and easy-to-implement architecture methodology. Using a self-created Enterprise Architecture Implementation Wheel, he developed an approach to implementing Enterprise Architecture that can be used by both novice and experienced architects.

Eric has been practicing Enterprise Architecture for over 15 years and has extensive knowledge and experience in the development and application of Enterprise Architecture. He easily leverages architecture to translate business strategy into implementation. Eric likes to focus on the practical and pragmatic application of Enterprise Architecture and lectures on Enterprise Architecture at the Eindhoven University of Technology. He also writes about his daily experiences in his blog: *eawheel.com/blog*.

About the Reviewer

 **Rob Malschaert** is an experienced Enterprise Architect, primarily working in the healthcare sector as an independent Enterprise Architect. Rob is certified in TOGAF and ArchiMate and is also a Certified Information Systems Security Professional (CISSP).

Rob has extensive experience in the practical application of Enterprise Architecture in complex organizations, especially in integrating *working under architecture* in organizations that are inexperienced in using architecture as a tool to achieve organizational objectives. Additionally, Rob actively contributes to the development of the Dutch Hospital Reference Architecture (ZiRA) and provides postgraduate-level education on Enterprise Architecture at the Eindhoven University of Technology.

Acknowledgments

First and foremost, I would like to thank my current and former employers for providing me with invaluable work environments and lecture opportunities that inspired me to write this book. The variety of situations there allowed me to envision and create an adapted architecture methodology that is illustrated in this book.

Special thanks go to Rob Malschaert, a former colleague of mine and my current partner in lecturing in the field of architecture at the Eindhoven University of Technology, for agreeing to be the reviewer for this book. His keen insight and attention to detail were essential in ensuring that the material is presented clearly.

I am also grateful for the support and advice of Whynde Kuehn, author of *Strategy to Reality*. Whynde also took the trouble to write the foreword for this book.

My thanks also go to the staff at Apress Media, who guided a first-time author through the writing and editing process with good-natured professionalism.

I would also like to thank Aditee Mirashi (Acquisitions Editor) for accepting my manuscript submission and going out of her way to answer all of my numerous questions prior to the publishing process.

Finally, I would like to thank my wife, Nienke, whose trust and support made this book possible.

Foreword

Is there anything more powerful than an idea? An idea is the kernel of all possibilities, with unlimited potential to change the world. Indeed, ideas have shaped all of our human history.

We are all familiar with the philosophical thought experiment: *If a tree falls in a forest and no one is around to hear it, does it make a sound?* Here's another one: *If an organization formulates the most brilliant strategy for competitive advantage but it never gets implemented, does it matter?* Or even: *If we develop the most brilliant framework to help organizations work more effectively but if they don't know how to apply it in practice, does it make an impact?*

What is more powerful than an idea then is an idea that is executed.

That is what this book is all about.

To survive and thrive, *organizations must do change well* in a world of increasing disruption and uncertainty. This applies to organizations of every size, industry, and sector – from Fortune Global 500 companies and governments to startups and non-profit organizations. Surprisingly though, organizations around the world continually struggle to execute strategies and business change in an effective, coordinated way at pace, and the statistics and stories abound that reflect this.

This is where *Enterprise Architecture* comes in.

After giving a pertinent and insightful history of Enterprise Architecture, Eric brings us to where the discipline has evolved today. As he states, "Enterprise Architecture has evolved from a primarily IT-focused discipline to a strategic and business-centric practice." We've come a long way, and the holistic view of Enterprise Architecture has never been more important than it is today.

Enterprise Architecture is a framework for understanding and managing the overall structure and strategy of an organization. This framework helps us design our organizations with intent for effectiveness, agility, and value as well as navigate complexity and inform business decision-making. Enterprise Architecture is also the often-missing *bridge between strategy and execution.* It plays a critical role in translating strategy into a coordinated set of actions that enables an organization to achieve its goals and objectives – and ensures the continual alignment of initiatives and investments back to business direction. Enterprise Architecture guides us to do the right things, at the right time, for the right reasons.

The intentional, agile design of an organization and its ability to execute strategy together create the ability to respond to change. Enterprise Architecture is critical to both.

This means that *organizations must do Enterprise Architecture well.*

This book is a reference and a guide for your journey of implementing Enterprise Architecture.

While Enterprise Architecture frameworks define **what** to do, they do not necessarily tell you **how** to do it. This book helps to bridge that gap. Through his depth of experience, Eric translates the theory of Enterprise Architecture frameworks into a practical set of steps and guidance, codified through his Implementation Wheel and demonstrated through an example company. This book accelerates you so that you can focus on doing what matters most: *applying* Enterprise Architecture within your organization to achieve the value for which it was intended.

Eric walks you through the process of implementing Enterprise Architecture with such specificity, care, and passion that it is like having your own personal guide. He unpacks the practical details you need to know to build out different aspects of Enterprise Architecture, including how to collaborate with others and facilitate effective conversations. He helps you adapt the sequence and approaches to your realities, gives expert tips, steers you around potential challenges, and shows you the way with an extensive set of examples and blueprints. He even tells stories along the way to entertain and educate.

Implementing Enterprise Architecture is a continual journey for every organization. The architecture itself is ever evolving and expanding with the business, but as the discipline is leveraged, it also shifts mindsets. Enterprise Architecture facilitates new ways of thinking and working around how organizations provide value, deliver strategic change, make decisions for the enterprise, and design for today and a future-ready tomorrow. Architecture and architectural thinking are beneficial for *everyone*, not just architects.

With some courage, patience, skill, and an expert guide to keep you on solid footing, a rewarding journey lies ahead. Whether you are experienced in Enterprise Architecture or new to the discipline, your next step to greater meaning and impact for your organization or career is contained here in these pages. Open your mind to all that Enterprise Architecture has become and can be as a strategic discipline critical to helping our organizations and societies meet their challenges and opportunities ahead with success.

All the best to you on the journey!

Whynde Kuehn
Author of *Strategy to Reality*
Founder and Managing Director
S2E Transformation Inc.

CHAPTER 1

Introduction

I have been practicing Enterprise Architecture for over 15 years.
During these years I have worked for several organizations. All of these
organizations presented unique situations, each requiring a slightly
different way of working.

The organizations did have one thing in common: architecture
maturity was either non-existent or at a low level. One of the main reasons
for this is probably (because we never really know for sure) the difficulty
an organization has in translating the available theoretical architecture
frameworks into a practical application.

Despite the good intentions of frameworks such as the TOGAF
Standard [1], there still are a lot of organizations that have not yet
been able to translate a framework into something that is usable. If an
organization could easily use the tools provided by a framework, working
with architecture would be more likely to get the attention it needs. An
organization would be able to greatly benefit from the structure and
coherence that a framework has to offer. In spite of the fact that the theory
described in the frameworks has evolved and matured over the years,
organizations have not yet found a way to put it to good use. I believe this
is because theoretical frameworks do not pay enough attention to the
pragmatic translation of their content into a practical application.

In this book, I want to take the reader on a journey I call *Getting Started
with Enterprise Architecture*. I have tried to take the theory from existing
frameworks and translate it into a practical and pragmatic approach.

© Eric Jager 2023
E. Jager, *Getting Started with Enterprise Architecture*,
https://doi.org/10.1007/978-1-4842-9858-9_1

With this approach, a basic implementation of Enterprise Architecture can be achieved. The method described in this book is based on the theory and methodology outlined in the TOGAF Standard. The book is written from the idea of the methodology, but does not apply it to the letter of the theory.

When you start implementing Enterprise Architecture, it's good to use one of the frameworks available. But such a framework can quickly feel a bit overwhelming. A framework describes in reasonable detail all the steps that can or should be taken to achieve a complete implementation of Enterprise Architecture.

However, it is not always necessary to follow all of these steps from start to finish. This is especially true for the detailed approach that the frameworks prescribe. If an organization has not yet integrated working with architecture into its day-to-day operations, there is certainly no need to follow the frameworks' approach to the letter. But how do you start, and what do you start with? What do you do and what don't you do? What do you do first, and what do you do next?

In this book, I provide both novice and experienced architects with a brief overview of Enterprise Architecture, explaining the origins of architecture, the most popular frameworks, and the architecture domains. The book then moves on to provide insight into the visualization of architecture by educating the reader on topics such as the architecture modeling language, essential architecture elements and concepts, and a place to store it all: the Architecture Repository.

After laying out the basics, the book continues with a deep dive into the self-developed Enterprise Architecture Implementation Wheel. The Implementation Wheel is based on the methodology described in the TOGAF Standard and provides architects with a method that is easy to use because of its practical and pragmatic approach to implementing Enterprise Architecture. Using the Enterprise Architecture Implementation Wheel, I will show you how to tailor an architecture framework to the implementation needs of the existing organization. I will also show you how to produce artifacts (architecture deliverables) that are useful and usable, and get you started with Enterprise Architecture.

The book concludes with a description of an actual architecture implementation that uses the Enterprise Architecture Implementation Wheel in practice.

Using the challenges faced by the fictional company Lemon-A-de, I will demonstrate how a basic Enterprise Architecture can be used to help an organization implement its intended strategy. Although Lemon-A-de is a relatively small organization, the power of applying Enterprise Architecture in translating strategy into execution becomes clear.

Enterprise Architecture can be implemented in many different ways. The way described in this book is just one of them. Following the steps outlined in this book, using the Enterprise Architecture Implementation Wheel, results in a usable whole and lays the foundation for further development of Enterprise Architecture within the organization.

Getting Started with Enterprise Architecture is the ideal handbook for the architect who is tasked with implementing Enterprise Architecture in an existing organization.

CHAPTER 2

Architecture Origin

This chapter describes the origins of Enterprise Architecture. What created the need for structure to which Enterprise Architecture proved to be the answer? A timeline is used to provide insight into the key events that led to the emergence, evolution, and maturation of architecture. Additionally, a brief explanation of the structure of the two best-known architecture frameworks (the Zachman Framework and the TOGAF Standard) is provided. As part of the TOGAF Standard, this chapter also introduces the Architecture Development Method. The chapter concludes with the similarities and differences between the two frameworks.

2.1. Timeline

The origins of Enterprise Architecture can be traced back to the 1960s and 1970s, when large organizations began to recognize the need for formal methods to manage and align their complex IT systems with business goals. During this time, there were various efforts to develop system architectures and information models.

In the 1980s, the term *Enterprise Architecture* began to gain traction. The focus was primarily on defining and documenting the structure and components of an organization's information systems. This decade saw the emergence of methodologies such as John Zachman's *Framework for Enterprise Architecture* [2]. Enterprise Architecture emerged as a response to the increasing complexity of IT environments and business processes.

© Eric Jager 2023
E. Jager, *Getting Started with Enterprise Architecture*,
https://doi.org/10.1007/978-1-4842-9858-9_2

The 1990s marked a period of increased interest and growth in the field of Enterprise Architecture. More and more organizations recognized the importance of aligning IT with business goals. The Open Group introduced the TOGAF Standard in 1995, providing a comprehensive approach to Enterprise Architecture.

The early 2000s saw a greater focus on integrating IT and business strategies, leading to the adoption of Enterprise Architecture as a *strategic management discipline.* Enterprise Architecture frameworks and methodologies, such as the Zachman Framework and the TOGAF Standard, gained wider acceptance and use. In the mid to late 2000s, Enterprise Architecture evolved to address the complexities of globalized and networked enterprises. The focus shifted to a more holistic approach to Enterprise Architecture, encompassing not only IT systems but also business processes, people, and organizational structures. This broader perspective was necessary to adapt to rapidly changing market dynamics and technological innovations.

The evolution of Enterprise Architecture brought a new focus to the *strategic importance* of IT within organizations. It provided a way to align IT infrastructure and business processes with business goals, thereby increasing the value of IT. Enterprise Architecture also offered a way to manage and reduce the complexity of IT environments, thereby reducing the cost and risk of IT projects.

In the 2010s, Enterprise Architecture became increasingly integrated with other strategic management disciplines, such as business process management, data management, and cybersecurity. Enterprise Architecture became an essential tool for guiding digital transformation initiatives, cloud adoption, and agile development practices.

In recent years, Enterprise Architecture has continued to evolve in response to the growing importance of digitization, data-driven decision-making, and emerging technologies such as artificial intelligence, the Internet of Things (IoT), and blockchain. Enterprise Architecture is becoming more adaptive and agile to address the dynamic and rapidly changing business landscape.

Today, organizations use Enterprise Architecture to optimize their business processes and IT infrastructure, accelerate their digital transformation, and strengthen their competitive position. Enterprise Architecture continues to evolve and adapt to the ever-changing technology environment and business needs.

Throughout its history, Enterprise Architecture has evolved from a primarily IT-focused discipline to a *strategic and business-centric practice*. It plays a critical role in helping organizations optimize their operations, align their IT investments with business goals, and navigate the complexities of the modern digital age. As technology and business needs continue to evolve, Enterprise Architecture will undoubtedly remain a critical discipline for organizations seeking competitive advantage and long-term success. Architectural frameworks have been developed to provide structure to the ever-evolving environment. These frameworks provide the guidance needed to manage the complexity of IT environments and business processes.

Over the years, several architecture frameworks have been developed. The most popular architecture frameworks are the Zachman Framework, the TOGAF Standard, and the BIZBOK Guide [8]. In addition to the development of frameworks, the architecture modeling language ArchiMate was also created (see Chapter 6, Section 6.2). The modeling language provided a solution for visualizing the complex environments of organizations. Over the past decades, the frameworks and the modeling language have continued to evolve and mature.

The evolution of the best-known architectural frameworks and the modeling language, starting with the introduction of the Zachman Framework [3], is shown in Table 2-1. Key milestones over the past 35 years are included in the overview. The overview is limited to milestones related to the Zachman Framework, the TOGAF Standard, the BIZBOK Guide, and ArchiMate.

Table 2-1. *Major events in the field of architecture*

Year	Event
1987	John Zachman publishes the Zachman Framework (with three columns)
1995	TOGAF (The Open Group Architecture Framework) is released
2001	ArchiMate, a modeling language for Enterprise Architectures, is released
	First publication of the Zachman Framework with all six columns
2007	TOGAF 8.1 is released, with enhanced support for SOA and IT management
2009	ArchiMate 1.0 is released
2011	TOGAF 9 is released, with enhanced support for business and IT alignment
	A 3.0 version of the Zachman Framework is published, labeled Enterprise Ontology instead of framework
	First release of the BIZBOK Guide
2012	ArchiMate 2.0 is released
2016	ArchiMate 3.0 is released
2018	TOGAF 9.2 is released, with enhanced support for digital transformation
2022	The Open Group releases The TOGAF Standard, 10th Edition, with support for agile architectures and new technologies such as AI and blockchain
	The BIZBOK Guide 11.0 is released
	ArchiMate 3.2 is released
2023	The BIZBOK Guide 12.0 is released

The BIZBOK Guide is a more limited framework than, for example, the Zachman Framework or the TOGAF Standard. The BIZBOK Guide focuses solely on Business Architecture. For this reason, the BIZBOK framework is not discussed further in this chapter.

2.2. Zachman Framework

The first architecture frameworks appeared in the 1980s and 1990s. The Zachman Framework, published by John Zachman in 1987, was the first framework (actually an ontology) that focused on structuring business processes and IT infrastructure.

Throughout the 1990s, the Zachman Framework became increasingly popular as an Enterprise Architecture methodology. The framework was used by many organizations, including large corporations and government agencies. During this time, the framework underwent several modifications to better meet the needs of organizations.

Shortly after the year 2000, the Zachman Framework was further developed, extended, and adapted to the changing needs of organizations. More attention was paid to the relationship between Enterprise Architecture and digital transformation, and new tools and techniques were developed to support Enterprise Architecture modeling. There have also been several discussions held about the applicability and practical value of the Zachman Framework and its role in an ever-changing IT environment [4].

The Zachman Framework provides a structured approach to understanding and managing organizational complexity through a matrix model. The framework defines a set of perspectives or *viewpoints* from different stakeholders and focuses on six fundamental questions: what, how, where, who, when, and why. Since 2001, these questions have been presented in a six-by-six matrix, with each column representing one of the perspectives and each row representing one of the questions (see Figure 2-1).

The framework emphasizes the importance of exploring each cell in the matrix to gain a complete understanding of the organization and its architecture. It encourages multidisciplinary collaboration and helps identify gaps, duplications, and inconsistencies within the architecture.

The framework is broadly applicable and can be used for different types of architecture, such as Business Architecture, Information Architecture, and Technology Architecture. It provides a structured approach to managing complexity and guiding the design and transformation of an organization.

	What	How	Where	Who	When	Why	
Planner							Scope
Owner							Concepts
Designer							Logic
Builder							Physics
Imple-menter							Technology
Operator							Product
	Material	Process	Geometry	Instructions	Timing	Objectives	

Figure 2-1. *The Zachman Framework in its most generic form*

The Zachman Framework is an ontology – a theory of the existence of a structured set of essential components of an object for which explicit expressions are necessary and perhaps even mandatory for creating, operating, and changing the object (the object being an enterprise, a department, a value chain, a "sliver," a solution, a project, an airplane, a building, a product, a profession, or whatever).

The Zachman Framework *is not* a methodology for creating the implementation (an instantiation) of the object. The framework *is* the ontology for describing the enterprise. The framework (ontology) is a *structure* whereas a methodology is a *process*. A structure is *not* a process. A structure establishes definition whereas a process provides transformation [2].

2.3. The Open Group Architecture Framework (TOGAF)

The TOGAF Standard, created in 1995 and further developed by The Open Group, is one of the best-known architecture frameworks, along with the Zachman Framework. The framework consists of several components, including an Architecture Development Method, a set of standards, and a set of tools and techniques. The TOGAF Standard is designed to help organizations develop a holistic and integrated Enterprise Architecture that is aligned with their business objectives.

The TOGAF Standard is widely used by large organizations and government agencies. The framework provides a structured approach to developing and implementing Enterprise Architecture. It also provides a common language and method for communicating architecture concepts and solutions. The TOGAF Standard is useful for increasing an organization's IT effectiveness by developing a robust, flexible, and interoperable IT infrastructure.

One of the key benefits of the TOGAF Standard is its wide acceptance and popularity within the industry. The framework is used by thousands of organizations around the world and has led to the development of an extensive ecosystem of tools, training, and certification programs.

It is often said that the TOGAF Standard is an IT architecture framework par excellence. Therefore, it would not be useful as an Enterprise Architecture framework. However, nothing could be further from the truth. Over several decades, the TOGAF Standard has become increasingly focused on Enterprise Architecture. Partly due to the introduction of improved support for business and IT alignment, the framework has evolved into a full-fledged Enterprise Architecture framework.

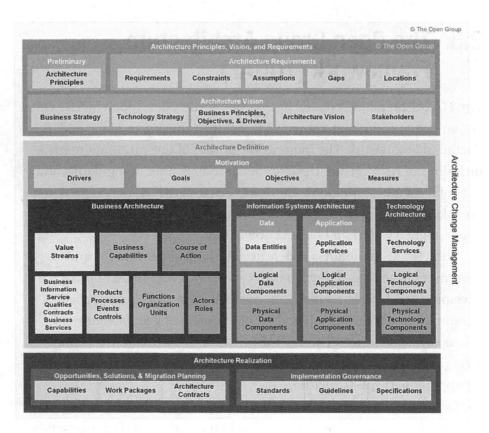

Figure 2-2. *TOGAF Architecture Content Framework*

The TOGAF Standard consists of several components that work together to provide a comprehensive Enterprise Architecture development method. The TOGAF Standard has two main components: *Fundamental Content* and *Series Guides*.

2.3.1. Fundamental Content

The Fundamental Content consists of six documents: Core Concepts, Architecture Development Method (ADM), ADM Techniques, Applying the ADM, Architecture Content and Enterprise Architecture Capability (Figure 2-3).

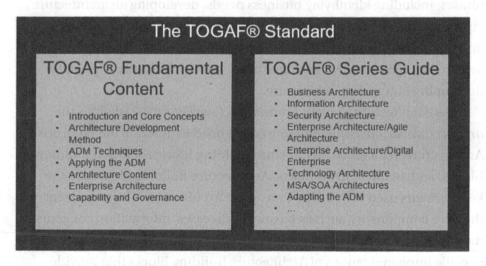

Figure 2-3. *The TOGAF Standard, 10th Edition*

As the name *Introduction and Core Concepts* suggests, this document describes the core concepts that are used throughout the components of the TOGAF Standard. This includes the definition of Enterprise Architecture (see Chapter 3) and the different Architecture Domains (see Chapter 4) that the TOGAF Standard distinguishes. The Architecture Development Method (see Section 2.3.1.1) is also briefly explained.

The ADM is discussed in more detail in the documents *Architecture Development Method (ADM)*, *ADM Techniques*, and *Applying the ADM*. The *Introduction and Core Concepts* document also consists of an explanation and use of deliverables, artifacts, and building blocks, as well as a brief mention of the Enterprise Continuum, the Architecture Repository, and the Content Framework. In fact, the *Core Concepts* document introduces a number of important topics but refers to other documents in the Fundamental Content for more detailed explanations.

The *Architecture Development Method* is the most important part of the TOGAF Standard. It is a step-by-step method for developing and implementing Enterprise Architecture. The ADM includes several phases, including identifying business needs, developing an architecture vision, creating an architecture plan, implementing the architecture, and maintaining the architecture. The TOGAF Standard is one of the few architecture frameworks that actually has a process description for developing Enterprise Architecture.

The Architecture Content Framework (see Figure 2-2) defines the *architectural artifacts* and *building blocks* used to describe the Enterprise Architecture. It includes Architecture Building Blocks, Solution Building Blocks, and architectural artifacts. Architecture Building Blocks are the key elements used to build the Enterprise Architecture. They represent the core components, such as business processes, information concepts, data entities, and application systems. Solution Building Blocks are specific implementations of Architecture Building Blocks that provide a concrete solution to a specific problem. Architectural artifacts are the deliverables produced during the phases of the Architecture Development Method, such as catalogs, matrices, diagrams, and maps that describe the architecture (see also Chapter 6, Section 6.3).

In addition to the building blocks, the Fundamental Content also includes the *Enterprise Continuum*. This is a classification system used to categorize architectural assets. It consists of two main parts, Foundation Architecture and Common System Architectures. The former provides a set of common systems, services, and standards that form the basis for an organization's specific architectures, while the latter represents industry reference models and standards that can be used as a basis for an organization's architecture development.

The Fundamental Content is further complemented by *reference models* and the *Architecture Capability Framework*. Reference models are pre-defined models that provide generic solutions to common architectural problems, whereas the Architecture Capability Framework outlines the organizational structure, roles, and processes needed to establish and operate an effective enterprise architecture capability within an organization.

Finally, a section that provides additional guidelines, techniques, and reference materials to support the effective use of the framework is called the TOGAF *Resource Base*. It provides guidance on how to tailor the TOGAF Standard to an organization's specific needs and requirements. Overall, the Fundamental Content of the TOGAF Standard serves as a comprehensive guide and toolbox for organizations to develop, manage, and evolve their Enterprise Architecture, promote alignment between IT and business strategies, and foster efficient and effective IT systems.

2.3.1.1. Architecture Development Method

The Architecture Development Method (Figure 2-4) is a key component of the TOGAF Standard. It is a comprehensive and iterative approach for developing and managing Enterprise Architectures. The ADM provides a step-by-step guide for creating and maintaining architecture artifacts and ensuring alignment with business goals. The ADM is considered a process that enables Enterprise Architects to develop and implement Enterprise Architecture.

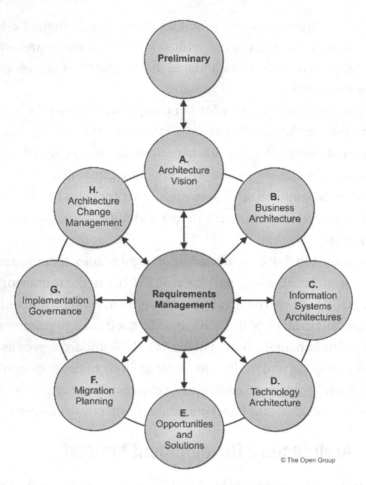

Figure 2-4. *The Architecture Development Method*

The phases of the ADM are as follows:

Preliminary Phase: The Preliminary Phase is the first phase of the ADM and lays the foundation for the architecture development process. It includes the establishment of the architecture project and the necessary supporting resources and governance. The primary objectives of this phase are to define the scope of the architecture effort and to define business scenarios, as well as to secure sponsorship and board approval.

Phase A: Architecture Vision. This phase is the initial starting point of the ADM and lays the foundation for the architecture project or implementation. It involves understanding the business drivers, goals, and objectives and creating an Architecture Vision that aligns with the strategic direction of the organization. Key activities include identifying stakeholders, defining the scope of the architecture, and developing a high-level business case. The output of this phase is the Architecture Vision document, which serves as a reference point throughout the ADM process.

Phase B: Business Architecture. In this phase, the focus shifts to understanding the Business Architecture of the organization. The primary objectives are to define the business functions, capabilities, and processes required to achieve the Architecture Vision. Enterprise Architects work with business stakeholders to gather information about the business strategy, structure, and operations. The output is the Business Architecture document, which includes business models, process flows, and capability maps.

Phase C: Information Systems Architecture. The purpose of the Information Systems Architecture phase is to develop a technology blueprint that supports the Business Architecture. It identifies the key information systems required to implement the business capabilities and defines the Data and Application Architectures. The architects assess the existing systems and determine the gaps that need to be addressed. Deliverables from this phase include data models, application portfolios, and technology standards.

Phase D: Technology Architecture. Building on the information gathered in the previous phases, the Technology Architecture phase focuses on defining the infrastructure and technology required to support the information systems. Architects consider factors such as hardware, software, networking, security, and integration requirements. The result is a comprehensive Technology Architecture document that provides guidelines for building and deploying the technology infrastructure.

Phase E: Opportunities and Solutions. The Opportunities and Solutions phase evaluates and selects the most appropriate solutions to address the gaps identified in the previous phases. Architects identify potential architecture options, perform a risk assessment, and recommend appropriate solutions to stakeholders. They consider both internal development and external sourcing options. The output of this phase is a set of architecture specifications and implementation plans.

Phase F: Migration Planning. In this phase, the architects focus on creating a detailed plan for implementing the selected solutions. They develop a step-by-step approach for transitioning from the current state to the target state architecture. This includes defining transition architectures and identifying critical milestones, resources, and timelines. The Migration Planning document provides the roadmap for the transformation journey.

Phase G: Implementation Governance. Implementation Governance is about establishing the mechanisms to oversee the execution of the architecture project. It involves defining the organizational structure, roles, and responsibilities to ensure that the architecture is implemented as intended. Architects work closely with project management teams to monitor progress and address any deviations from the plan. The result is a governance framework that helps manage risk and ensures alignment with the Architecture Vision.

Phase H: Architecture Change Management. Architecture is not static, and the environment in which it operates evolves over time. The Architecture Change Management phase is concerned with managing changes to the architecture throughout its life cycle. It includes assessing the impact of changes, defining procedures for making changes, and ensuring that the architecture remains aligned with business goals.

Requirements Management: Although not considered a separate phase, Requirements Management is a continuous activity that runs throughout the ADM. It involves managing and maintaining requirements and ensuring that they are properly addressed during each phase. As the architecture evolves, new requirements may emerge, and existing requirements may change. Effective Requirements Management ensures that the final architecture meets all the necessary criteria.

The ADM is *iterative* in nature, meaning that each phase can be revisited as needed. Architects continually evaluate and refine the architecture as they move through the phases, ensuring that it remains relevant and effective. The end result is a comprehensive and well-aligned Enterprise Architecture that supports the organization's business goals.

The stages of the Enterprise Architecture Implementation Wheel described in this book (Figure 8-1) align with the various phases of the ADM. Refer to Chapter 8, Table 8-1, for an overview of the mapping.

2.3.2. Series Guides

The TOGAF Series Guides were developed in response to the need for more and better guidance on how to develop a more useful Enterprise Architecture. Stakeholders want useful Enterprise Architecture guidance to support their decisions and guide the implementation of necessary organizational changes.

The TOGAF Series Guides cover a range of topics, from general guidance on how to set up an Enterprise Architecture team, to domain-specific material for Business and Security Architecture, to using Agile methods and Agile software development. An approach to developing Enterprise Architecture following the Architecture Development Method provides guidance on using the framework to develop, maintain, and use an Enterprise Architecture. It is a companion to the Fundamental Content and brings the concepts and generic constructs to life. Other guides offer insights into using the TOGAF Standard in the digital enterprise, emphasizing how to establish and enhance an Enterprise Architecture capability that is aligned with the organization and what the Enterprise Architecture team is expected to support.

The TOGAF Series Guides also include:

- Domain-specific guidance, such as integrating risk and security into an Enterprise Architecture.

- A foundation for understanding and using business models.

- An explanation of what business capabilities are and how to use them to improve business analysis and planning.

- Details on how business scenarios can develop resonant business requirements and how they support and enable the organization to achieve its business goals.

In addition, the Series Guides describe how to apply the Architecture Development Method in an Agile delivery environment by breaking an architecture development project into small time-boxed increments and applying common Agile techniques. Finally, it provides reference models, techniques for assessing and quantifying an organization's Enterprise Architecture maturity, and documents that provide guidance on using project management techniques to manage the development of the Enterprise Architecture.

2.4. Similarities and Differences

Although the Zachman Framework and the TOGAF Standard have different approaches to Enterprise Architecture, they also have some similarities. For instance, both frameworks propose a structured approach to modeling an organization, and they both aim to create a holistic view of the organization that considers all of its key aspects.

An important difference between these frameworks is their *focus*. The Zachman Framework emphasizes the six perspectives and six aspects of the organization, while the TOGAF Standard covers a broader range of topics, including technology, applications, and information systems. The Zachman Framework is, therefore, suitable for organizations with a strong focus on business processes and business rules. The TOGAF Standard, on the other hand, is better suited for organizations that also have a need to manage complex technology environments.

Lastly, the TOGAF Standard provides a process for developing architecture, whereas most other frameworks do not. The process for developing architecture is called the Architecture Development Method and is briefly illustrated in Section 2.3.1.1.

2.5. Summary

Chapter 2 described the origins of Enterprise Architecture.

- A timeline was provided to illustrate the import events that led to the emergence, evolution, and maturity of the field of architecture.

- The two best-known architecture frameworks (the Zachman Framework and the TOGAF Standard) were explained, and the structure of both frameworks, as well as the Architecture Development Method, was briefly discussed.

- The chapter concluded with the similarities and differences between the two frameworks.

CHAPTER 3

Architecture Definition

In Chapter 3, the definition of architecture is given. We learn that there are several definitions and that each interpretation of the field has a different point of view. The various definitions are all correct in themselves, even though they differ slightly from each other. Giving an unambiguous definition of architecture turns out to be not so easy.

3.1. Defining Enterprise Architecture

Ask someone to describe an apple. Nine times out of ten, the person will come up with something like it is *a round piece of fruit with a stem (and a small leaf) that contains vitamins*. Some will also add a color to the description. But the description could just as easily refer to a cherry, or a grape. Granted, cherries and grapes are also fruits, but they are not apples. To avoid *comparing apples and oranges*, definitions are used.

To this day, there are different views on the definition of Enterprise Architecture. It seems that no single definition can be given to the field. It even happens that several definitions are used within the same framework, depending on the context [5].

The TOGAF Standard adopts the ISO/IEC/IEEE 42010:2011 standard for defining Enterprise Architecture but leaves room for additional interpretation.

© Eric Jager 2023
E. Jager, *Getting Started with Enterprise Architecture*,
https://doi.org/10.1007/978-1-4842-9858-9_3

The fundamental concepts or properties of a system in its environment embodied in its elements, relationships, and in the principles of its design and evolution [6].

The Open Group's framework has added the following to the above definition, which it says depends on the context.

The structure of components, their inter-relationships, and the principles and guidelines governing their design and evolution over time [7].

Both definitions are obviously correct in content, but difficult to read and understand for an organization beginning to develop Enterprise Architecture. The following definition is self-conceived and uses simpler language to explain what the essence of Enterprise Architecture is and includes.

Enterprise Architecture is a framework for understanding and managing the overall structure and strategy of an organization.

Enterprise Architecture is about creating a holistic view of the organization's activities, including its business processes, information systems, and technology infrastructure.

The purpose of Enterprise Architecture is to align these various elements with the goals and objectives of the organization and to ensure that the elements work together effectively and efficiently.

Enterprise Architecture focuses on identifying and resolving inconsistencies in business operations and enables planning for future growth and development.

This definition is a further and more comprehensive explanation of what the TOGAF Standard prescribes. Describing and articulating the definition more fully helps to understand exactly what is meant by Enterprise Architecture.

Where the definition talks about the *overall structure and strategy of an organization*, it clarifies that Enterprise Architecture is more than a field that focuses exclusively on an organization's IT systems. The phrase *creating a holistic view of the organization's activities* indicates that Enterprise Architecture takes on an organization-wide view. All activities supported by business processes, information systems, and technology infrastructure are interrelated. The next important point is the reference to *[aligning] with the goals and objectives of the organization*. This indicates that all activities performed by an organization, and all business processes, information systems, and technology infrastructure used in the process must be aligned with the organization's objectives. Finally, Enterprise Architecture should be used to *identify and resolve inconsistencies* so that the achievement of objectives is not compromised. It is also used to *plan for future growth and development* of the organization.

Enterprise Architecture is first and foremost about enabling an organization to achieve its goals and objectives, thereby realizing the organization's strategy. It is used to address stakeholder concerns and answer any questions they may have regarding the organization's portfolio or specific projects.

IT Architecture, on the other hand, is more technical in nature compared to Enterprise Architecture. Therefore, the two are miles apart from being the same. There is absolutely nothing technical to Enterprise Architecture. Diagrams and matrices (often referred to as technical in nature) are used to answer stakeholders' questions and address their concerns, not to illustrate technical solutions.

Enterprise Architecture oversees all the architecture domains (of which Technology Architecture is one) and plays a coordinating role. It leaves the execution of Technology Architecture to the IT Architects. As such, Enterprise Architecture is considered a strategic business management tool, not a technical instrument.

3.2. Summary

Chapter 3 discussed the definition of architecture that was given.

- The importance of having a clear definition was touched upon in this regard.

- It was also noted that multiple definitions exist and that each interpretation of the discipline is viewed from a different point of view.

CHAPTER 4

Architecture Domains

The present chapter discusses and explains the existence of and difference
between architecture layers and domains. The importance of information
concepts is discussed as the main factor for the introduction of an additional
architecture domain: Information Architecture.

4.1. Domains and Layers

The field of architecture has matured over the years. The evolution and
application of architecture frameworks has contributed to this. Today,
more and more organizations are recognizing the value of architecture.
Many of these organizations have hired architects to bring structure,
coherence, and consistency to the way information systems are deployed,
business processes are executed, and strategy is implemented. However,
hiring an architect does not mean that the rest will take care of itself.

The Enterprise Architect plays a critical role in establishing, applying,
and evolving Enterprise Architecture. However, the organization itself
is not exempt from making a significant contribution. In fact, it is the
organization's responsibility, in many areas. It is up to the organization to
define its strategy and to work with the architect to turn it into a realizable
implementation. Chapter 8, Section 8.3.3, describes how Enterprise
Architecture can help shape drivers, goals, objectives, and initiatives.
Section 8.4.1 takes a closer look at translating strategy into execution. Both
sections show that organizational participation in the architecture process
is essential.

© Eric Jager 2023
E. Jager, *Getting Started with Enterprise Architecture*,
https://doi.org/10.1007/978-1-4842-9858-9_4

Of course, the organization is not always involved at the level of translating strategy into execution. There are also situations and challenges that an Enterprise Architect can address on his or her own. In fact, there are many circumstances in which information must be gathered in order to take the first step toward implementing a basic Enterprise Architecture.

Many of these scenarios touch on the various facets of an organization. They may involve organizational design, processes, and the information used. The application landscape (what applications does the organization use) is also important, as is the technology used. Gathering information on these topics is one of the primary tasks of the architect. These aspects, which interface with different parts of the organization, are called *architecture domains*.

What began in Enterprise Architecture around the year 1990 – and was then still in the technology corner – has managed to evolve over the decades into a very mature field. A field that now covers all *aspects* of an organization. These aspects are referred to as *architectures* or *architecture domains*. For years it has been common to conflate architecture domains and layers, but the two are distinct enough.

Architecture layers refer to the logical divisions of a software system or application based on the *functionality* they provide. Each layer is responsible for a specific aspect of the system and communicates with adjacent layers through predefined interfaces. Common layers in a typical software architecture include presentation (user interface), business logic, and data storage. Separating the system into layers promotes modularity, maintainability, and reusability.

Architecture domains, on the other hand, are broader divisions that categorize different aspects of the overall system architecture. They represent the *areas of concern or expertise* that architects need to address while designing a complex system. Examples of architecture domains include Business and Information Architecture, Application Architecture, and Technology Architecture. Security Architecture is also considered to be an architecture domain. Each domain focuses on specific concerns and constraints related to its area and contributes to the overall design of the system.

Architecture layers focus on organizing the components and functionality of a system, while architecture domains categorize different concerns and perspectives that must be considered during the architectural design process. They are complementary concepts used to create well-structured and comprehensive software and system architectures.

The TOGAF Standard assumes three architecture domains (Figure 4-1): Business Architecture, Information Systems Architectures, and Technology Architecture. The domain in the middle, the Information Systems Architectures, consists of two parts. The first part focuses on data and deals with data entities, logical and physical data components. The second part of the Information Systems Architectures deals with applications. What is striking, especially given its name, is that the Information Systems Architectures domain does not mention an essential architectural concept, namely, *information*.

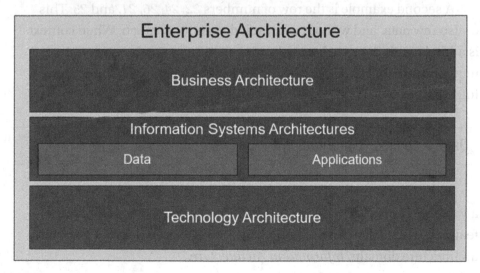

Figure 4-1. *The TOGAF Standard architecture domains*

4.2. The Information Domain

The framework (or standard) that does address the concept of information is the BIZBOK Guide [8]. This *Business Architecture Body of Knowledge* recognizes the importance of information. From this standard, information concepts are introduced. Information concepts are described in much more detail in the BIZBOK Guide than data entities are in the TOGAF Standard. Data entities have less granularity than information concepts. Aside from the difference between data and information, this makes the two concepts incomparable.

The reason this book uses information concepts is twofold. First, because of the much more comprehensive description of the concept in the BIZBOK Guide, and second, because data is something different from information. Data by itself does not have sufficient meaning. This means that raw data without context has little added value. To give an example, the address *1 Primary Lane* is meaningless by itself. Without context, little can be done with it. Adding the context of *the President's home address* to 1 Primary Lane gives meaning to the raw data.

A second example is the row of numbers *22, 24, 26, 21*, and *23*. This is also raw data, and without context it does not say much. When context is added to this data, such as indicating that these are the expected temperatures for next week, the data becomes meaningful. It becomes information.

Data + context = information

The two examples show that information (data placed in context) is a valuable concept. Therefore, information concepts are prominently featured in the following chapters. These concepts are located in a fourth architecture domain, *Information Architecture*.

4.3. Multi-domain Model

There are also views that suggest that there are as many as five domains. In these five-domain models, the Business Architecture domain is divided into two parts: an *organizational* part and a *process* part. The Information Systems Architectures domain from the TOGAF Standard is also divided into two parts. There is an *information* part and a *data/application* part. Where the TOGAF Standard distinguishes between data and applications, Business Architecture is very clear about the difference between information on the one hand and data and applications on the other. The fifth and final domain is *technology*. Figure 4-2 shows the five domains.

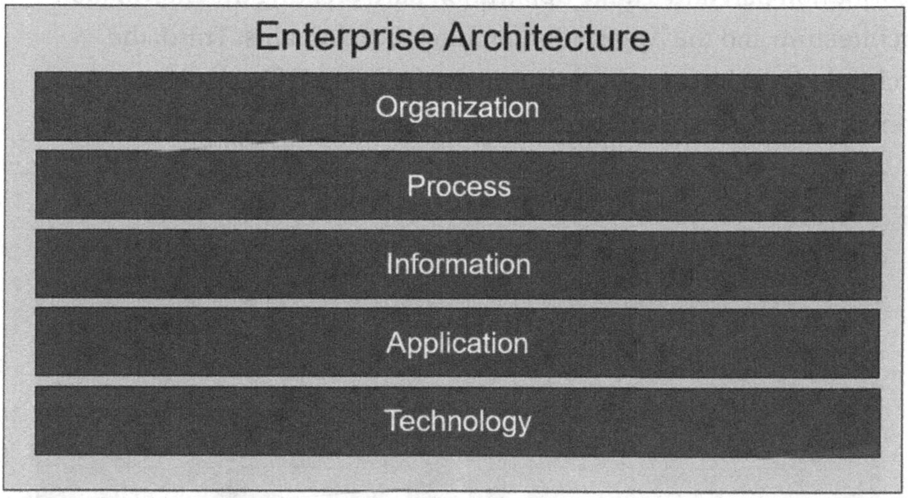

Figure 4-2. *Five-domain architecture model*

Personally, I think that a division into four architecture domains is still the best. The Business Architecture domain consists of organizational and process concepts; the Information Architecture domain contains information concepts. The Application Architecture domain provides applications and data objects, and the Technology Architecture domain consists of technology components.

Based on these four architecture domains, I believe that the TOGAF Standard could benefit from the addition of an essential architecture domain, Information Architecture.

Ultimately, there is no one final or correct way to look at the domains of Enterprise Architecture. The views presented here are illustrative. Everyone is free to adopt the view that suits them best.

This book uses and expands upon the three architecture domains of the TOGAF Standard. First, there is the Business Architecture domain. Second, the Information Systems Architectures domain is divided into an *information* part and a *data/application* part, creating the Information Architecture and the Application Architecture domains. Third, the Technology Architecture domain closes the ranks. This results in a four-domain Enterprise Architecture model (Figure 4-3).

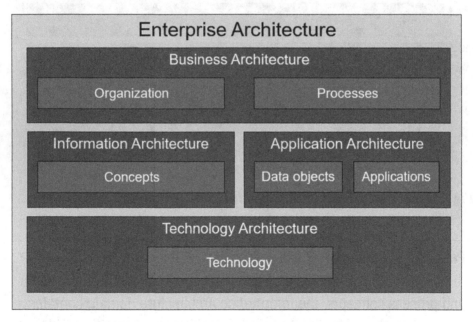

Figure 4-3. *Model with four architecture domains*

Figure 4-3 shows a layout of an Enterprise Architecture consisting of the aforementioned four domains. Each of these architectures has architectural elements that are specific to that domain. The basic elements associated with the four architecture domains that are used in this book are described in Chapter 6, Section 6.2.1.

4.4. Summary

Chapter 4 discussed the existence of and difference between architectural layers and domains.

- The importance of information concepts was seen as a major factor in introducing Information Architecture as an additional architecture domain.

CHAPTER 5

Architecture Roles

This next chapter examines the growth of the profession and the relationship of that growth to the emergence of the motley collection of architecture roles and functions. The function of the Enterprise Architect is described in more detail, and the similarities between this function and that of the Business Architect are noted. Other architecture roles and functions are briefly reviewed to give an idea of the variety that has emerged over the years.

5.1. Defining Roles and Functions

Within the field of architecture, there is still some confusion about the roles and functions of architects. For example, is a Technical Architect a role or a function? And what about an Application Architect or a Business Architect? And the Enterprise Architect, is that a role or a function, or maybe both? To end this ambiguity, it is helpful to take a look at the difference between roles and functions, and then classify the various names of architecture positions into the appropriate category.

The difference between a role and a function can be described as follows. *Roles* are linked to the *work processes* that are performed, unlike *functions*, which are much more linked to the *hierarchical structure* of the organization. Staying in the context of architecture, an architect may be assigned the role of Domain Architect, where in practice the person performs the function of a Technical Architect (based on a more general job description) within the hierarchy of the organization. To clarify, the

E. Jager, *Getting Started with Enterprise Architecture*,
https://doi.org/10.1007/978-1-4842-9858-9_5

person assigned to the *role* of Domain Architect is responsible for all work processes related to a specific domain. The *function* assigned to this person, that of a Technical Architect, allows the organization to place this person hierarchically with the IT department. If the function assigned to the person were that of a Business Architect, the hierarchical position would not be with an IT department, but rather with another business unit. In both situations, the role assigned to the person would still be that of a Domain Architect.

5.2. Generic Roles

Within the field of architecture, there are several generic architecture roles. These roles are shown schematically in Figure 5-1 and provide a high-level overview.

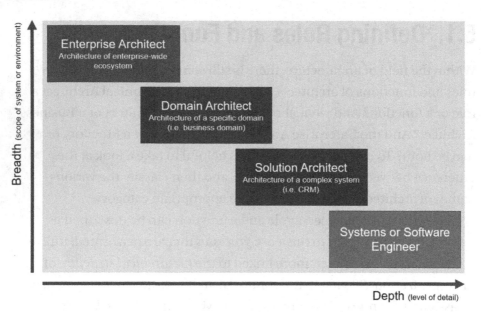

Figure 5-1. *Overview of generic architecture roles*

The roles differ in a number of ways. One is the scope of the system or environment to which the architecture applies (architecture *breadth*), and the other is the level of detail of the architecture (architecture *depth*). Four different roles exist [9]:

Enterprise Architect: This role is responsible for the entire and enterprise-wide ecosystem. In practice, however, the Enterprise Architect may specialize in a particular part of the enterprise. This is usually the case when an organization has several Enterprise Architects at its disposal. Like all other architecture roles, Enterprise Architects are part of the architecture capability. This capability focuses on all aspects relevant to Enterprise Architecture.

Domain Architect: A Domain Architect is responsible for a specific area (called a domain) below the enterprise level. For example, in a large organization, it is common for a Domain Architect to be responsible for everything related to a specific domain, such as the business domain (which includes business functions, business processes, business objects, etc.) or the information domain (which includes information concepts).

Solution Architect: The Solution Architect focuses specifically on a complex application or infrastructure element. For example, consider flagship applications such as a Customer Relationship Management application. Often, such an application has evolved over the years into a mix of legacy and modern components. As a result, in many cases it has become an extraordinarily complex environment. It is the Solution Architect's job to maintain the reliability of such a flagship application by ensuring that it remains cost-effective, user-friendly, secure, and future-proof.

Systems or Software Engineer: This last role is obviously not an architecture role. However, in some organizations, this role is given the title of IT Architect or Software Architect. It is then often held by a more senior engineer. The role of the Systems or Software Engineer is the most technical and detailed in nature and covers the lower right corner of Figure 5-1. Regardless of the name, it is a very important role, and that is why it is mentioned here. The role of a Systems or Software Engineer cannot be overlooked, because from an architect's perspective, these engineers are critical in enabling the realization of the system. They are tasked with specifying, implementing, and testing the functionality needed for a business application or infrastructure system. Valued for their expertise, System or Software Engineers provide feedback on architectural decisions. Unlike the Solution Architect, engineers focus on one part of the solution, while the architect's responsibility is to address the entire solution and the dependencies between components.

In summary, Enterprise Architects design, specify, implement, and evaluate the architecture of the entire enterprise ecosystem. Domain Architects perform the same steps at their level, and Solution Architects do so at the solution level.

5.3. Variety in Functions

Now, the management and administration of all architecture domains is the responsibility of the Enterprise Architect. However, several other architecture functions have emerged over the years. In part, this is due to the broad scope and responsibilities of the Enterprise Architect. In large organizations, it quickly became impossible for an Enterprise Architect to handle all the initiatives that span all the architecture domains. In order to still provide each of these architectures with appropriate attention, several complementary architecture functions have emerged over the years. For example, consider the function of the *Business Architect* or the *Application Architect* (both functions are variations of the Domain Architect role). The former is primarily focused on Business Architecture, while the latter is focused on activities within the Application Architecture domain.

The best known functions are those of the *Technical Architect* and *Software Architect*. Along with the Enterprise Architect function, these three are no longer the only ones. The changing demands of the marketplace and the world around us have resulted in the need for more architecture functions to continue to manage increasing levels of complexity across a diverse playing field.

In the 1990s, the position of Security Architect took off with the rise of the Internet, other digital channels, and the importance of maintaining control over data and activities. Another example of a relatively new function is the Cloud Architect. This function emerged in the early 2000s. At that time, cloud computing was becoming increasingly popular as an alternative to traditional on-premises IT infrastructure. With the rise of cloud computing, organizations were able to consolidate and centralize their IT services, resulting in significant cost savings and efficiencies.

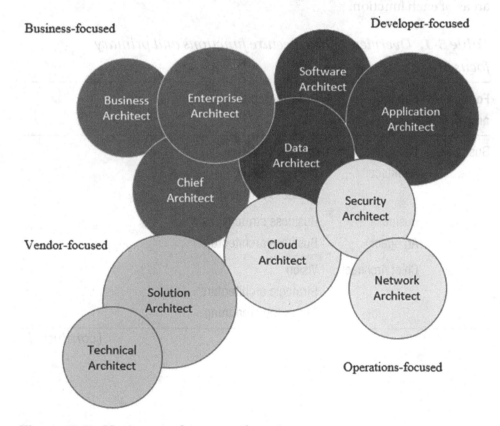

Figure 5-2. *Various architecture functions*

Figure 5-2 shows the variety of functions that have been created over the years. The different architecture functions all have their own focus area and are all variations of the Domain Architect role. They are fairly easy to group together. First, there is the *Business focus group*. This group includes the Enterprise Architect, Business Architect, and Chief Architect functions. The *Developer focus group* includes the Software Architect, Data Architect, and Application Architect functions. The Technical Architect and Solution Architect functions are located in the *Vendor focus group*. Finally, the *Operations focus group* includes the Cloud Architect, Security Architect, and Network Architect functions. Table 5-1 provides a schematic overview of the existing architecture functions and also shows the primary focus areas of each function.

Table 5-1. *Overview of architecture functions and primary focus areas*

Focus area	Function	Primary focus area
Business	Enterprise Architect	Business strategy
		Business goals
		Business architecture
	Business Architect	Business strategy
		Business architecture
	Chief Architect	Vision
		Strategic architecture
		Technology roadmap

(*continued*)

Table 5-1. (*continued*)

Focus area	Function	Primary focus area
Developer	Software Architect	Design of complex systems and applications Technical specifications Consistency and quality of software architecture
	Data Architect	Solutions for big data storage and processing Data lakes and data warehouses Use of advanced analysis tools and technologies
	Application Architect	Technology strategy Application life cycle
Vendor	Solution Architect	Technology strategy Life cycle of solutions
	Technical Architect	Technology strategy Life cycle of technology solutions
Operations	Security Architect	IT security strategy Life cycle of security solutions Meeting the changing threat environment and data protection legislation
	Cloud Architect	Cloud strategy Life cycle of cloud solutions
	Network Architect	Network strategy Life cycle of networks

The Enterprise Architect plays an important role in this book. It is this role and function that is responsible for implementing Enterprise Architecture. Therefore, this book describes the architecture-related activities from an Enterprise Architect's perspective.

5.4. The Enterprise Architect

The role and function of the Enterprise Architect originated in the 1990s, when companies began to realize that managing their IT infrastructure was becoming more complex as technologies evolved and organizations grew. Enterprise Architecture emerged as a way to integrate and streamline the various aspects of an organization, particularly business strategy, business processes, and technology. Today, it is referred to as *business and IT alignment*. Organizations have realized that a holistic view of their business structure and processes can help them to manage and integrate their IT infrastructure more efficiently and effectively. As a result, today's Enterprise Architects play an important role in developing and implementing IT strategies and systems that support business goals and objectives.

An Enterprise Architect is a professional who is responsible for designing, implementing, and managing an organization's Enterprise Architecture to support business goals and optimize business performance. This person works with the board of directors, executive team, and senior management to understand and translate the business strategy into Enterprise Architecture that enables the achievement of the goals and objectives. The Enterprise Architect is responsible for creating a holistic view of business processes, information systems, business data, and technologies to ensure that they work together seamlessly to support business objectives. This includes identifying key business processes and requirements, determining data needs, and designing the systems needed to support these processes.

An Enterprise Architect has a combination of business, IT, and project management skills. He or she must have a good understanding of business processes, needs, goals, and objectives, as well as a good understanding of the technologies needed to support those processes. An Enterprise Architect must also be able to communicate effectively with stakeholders from different disciplines and levels of the organization. The functions of Enterprise Architect and Business Architect are closely related and overlap in many areas. Both an Enterprise Architect and a Business Architect have the following responsibilities:

- Identifying critical business processes and determining data needs.

- Developing processes and systems to improve business performance.

- Identifying and solving business problems and providing solutions to improve performance.

- Working with stakeholders to understand and translate business strategy into an Enterprise Architecture.

- Working with IT teams to implement Enterprise Architecture.

- Keeping up with changes in the business environment and adjusting the business architecture as needed.

A Business Architect focuses on developing an Enterprise Architecture that supports business objectives. An Enterprise Architect ensures the development of a holistic view of the organization's business processes, information systems, business data, and technologies, as well as the development of governance frameworks. This ensures that Enterprise Architecture is consistently implemented and maintained. An Enterprise Architect is also responsible for identifying emerging technologies and trends relevant to the organization and advising senior management on their application.

To properly serve the organization, it is important to assume the appropriate architecture role. Therefore, it is necessary to have a clear picture of the organization's expectations and desires regarding the interpretation and execution of the architecture role.

I have seen many times in the past that there is a disconnect between what the organization expects an architect to do, or should do, and how the architect actually fills the position.

Several years ago, I worked for a hospital. In that hospital, I was dealing with an executive who was primarily looking for someone who could address the security concerns. All sorts of things that had a relationship (however limited) to security issues were put on my plate.

The executive was obviously looking for a Security Architect, but forgot that a Security Architect alone could not answer enterprise-wide questions. The Enterprise Architect role was not filled. Since security is a cross-cutting concern – and therefore can only exist if all other architectural domains are fleshed out – the role of Enterprise Architect had to be created.

At that time, I opted to fill the role of Enterprise Architect myself. One of the first things I did was to gather a group of people around me who could help me with the various issues that came up.

For the security-related issues, I found an experienced Security Engineer who was willing to take on that role. In this way, I was able to satisfy the manager's desire to address various security issues, and I also created space for myself to take on the role of Enterprise Architect so that issues could be addressed across the organization.

Personal expectations and interpretations of the architecture role may be very different from those of the organization. It is very important that both views are aligned. There should be no divergent views. Deploying the right architecture role is as important as positioning the architecture capability within the organization. Chapter 7 discusses the positioning of the architecture capability in more detail.

5.5. Summary

Chapter 5 examined the growth of the profession and the relationship of that growth to the emergence of the motley collection of architecture roles.

- The function of the Enterprise Architect was described in detail, and the similarities between this function and that of the Business Architect were identified.

- Other architecture roles and functions were reviewed as well, providing an overview of the diversity that has emerged over the years.

Architecture Visualization

This chapter focuses on visualizing the architecture. In order to communicate with the organization and its stakeholders, it is necessary to use a common language. This emphasizes the importance of consistency in the method of communication, as well as the use of uniformity. To achieve this, a unified modeling language must be used when visualizing architectural models and diagrams.

Chapter 6 also discusses the origins of the modeling language and identifies and explains the architectural elements used in this book. The architecture products (deliverables) catalog, matrix, diagram, and map are discussed, and the importance of using a good architecture tool is emphasized. Finally, the need for an architecture repository is addressed, and reasons are given why products such as an office suite are inadequate.

6.1. Language to Visualize

When it comes to communicating with and about the organization, two things are important: *unambiguous language* and the use of *visualizations*.

It is important to use a consistent and clear language when communicating the Enterprise Architecture to stakeholders. The organization's key players must play an active role in implementing

© Eric Jager 2023
E. Jager, *Getting Started with Enterprise Architecture*,
https://doi.org/10.1007/978-1-4842-9858-9_6

and evolving the Enterprise Architecture. To achieve good cooperation between the Enterprise Architect and the organization, it is essential to speak the same language so that both parties understand each other well.

Visualizing the Enterprise Architecture also plays an important role in communicating to the organization and its stakeholders. It is especially important to be able to create architecture models that are easy to read and understand. A picture (or in the case of architecture, a diagram) is often worth a thousand words. There is a reason for this saying, as it holds a grain of truth. By using architecture diagrams that are easy to read, the Enterprise Architect can convey certain messages or make complex situations understandable. The use of a uniform modeling language is an absolute necessity to achieve this goal.

6.2. Modeling Language

In order to capture and visualize an organization from an architectural perspective, the use of a modeling language is indispensable. In the context of architecture, this language is called ArchiMate. ArchiMate is a globally accepted standard for the visualization of architectural products. It is a modeling language designed to support the visualization, analysis, and communication of Enterprise Architectures. It was born out of the need for a standardized language to model complex Enterprise Architectures and IT systems.

The development of ArchiMate started in 2002 by a partnership of several Dutch public and private organizations, including the Dutch Tax Administration, Radboud University, and the Centrum Wiskunde & Informatica (CWI). These parties were responsible for the initial research into creating a general language for describing the development, maintenance, and operationalization of organizational structures, business processes, information flows and systems, and technical infrastructure. At that time, the language was based on IEEE standard 1471 [10]. This standard was adopted by the International Organization for Standardization (ISO) in 2007 as ISO/IEC 42010:2007. In 2011, it was superseded by the ISO/IEC/IEEE 42010.

The management and further development of ArchiMate was transferred to The Open Group in 2008. Since then, they have been managing and supporting ArchiMate as an open standard. In 2009, the first version of ArchiMate was released, called ArchiMate 1.0. This version provided a set of symbols and notations to model various aspects of Enterprise Architecture and IT systems. ArchiMate 1.0 focused on modeling the structure, behavior, and coherence of systems. Since the introduction of ArchiMate 1.0, several updates and enhancements have been made. These updates were based on user feedback and the continuing evolution of the field. ArchiMate 2.0 was introduced in 2012 and added several new concepts, including the ability to model motivation and organizational strategies. Version 3.0 followed in 2016.

Version 3.2 of the modeling language, introduced in 2023, extends the language and provides more capabilities for modeling the relationship between Business Architecture, Information Architecture, and Technology Architecture. It also allows for better integration with other architecture frameworks and standards. Figure 6-1 shows the integration of ArchiMate with the TOGAF Standard, specifically the Architecture Development Method.

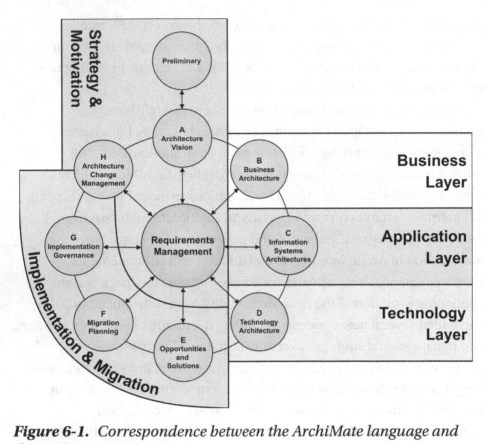

Figure 6-1. *Correspondence between the ArchiMate language and the TOGAF ADM*

Today, ArchiMate is used worldwide by architects, organizations, and consultants to model and visualize complex architectures. It has become an important tool in the field of Enterprise Architecture, helping to understand and communicate the structure and operation of organizations. The wide acceptance of ArchiMate as a standardized architecture modeling language has contributed to its growth and maturity. It is recognized as a highly valuable tool for planning, designing, and managing complex architectures.

The strength of the modeling language lies in the areas of uniformity and consistency. This applies mainly to the language's architectural elements and their design. The use of a standard color palette also contributes to the sense of uniformity. Although the modeling language uses yellow for the business operation layer, blue for the application layer, and green for the technology layer, the modeling language itself is colorless and completely color independent. The suggested colors are optional.

When the language was developed, the idea was to color the behavioral elements, such as business process and business service, as well as application service and technology service, yellow. Blue was used for the active elements such as business actor and business role, as well as application component and device. Finally, green was the color assigned to the passive elements. These include business objects, data objects, and artifacts.

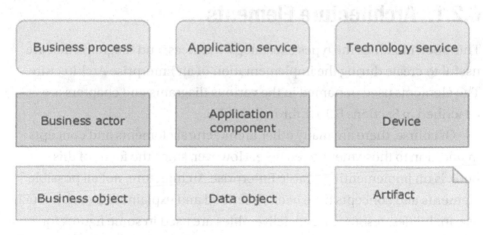

Figure 6-2.   *Original ArchiMate coloring*

Due to a problem with color assignment later in the development of ArchiMate, a different color application was used. This problem manifested itself when using elements such as interfaces and data/business objects. These elements all have the same shape. This was also true for functions and processes; business functions, application functions, and technology functions all share the same form with business processes, application processes, and technology processes. If these elements were used together in the same architecture view, it would not be possible to sufficiently distinguish between the elements used. Therefore, it was decided to use the colors at the architecture domain level. Yellow was used for Business Architecture, blue for Application Architecture, and green for Technology Architecture [11].

Disciplined use of colors is recommended. A changing color palette does not contribute to the uniformity of the models and diagrams to be used. It is, therefore, advisable to choose a standard color palette and stick to it, to avoid extra work and ambiguity. This will benefit the uniformity of the language.

6.2.1. Architecture Elements

This book identifies the types of catalogs, matrices, and diagrams that are useful to create during the implementation of an Enterprise Architecture. The elements used or named in the various diagrams and chapters are described in Sections 6.2.1.1 through 6.2.1.8.

Of course, there are many other architectural elements and concepts in addition to those mentioned here. However, since the focus of this book is on implementing a basic Enterprise Architecture, not all possible elements and concepts have been described and explained. Elements such as capabilities, resources, and deliverables are used in some figures for illustration and inspiration only.

6.2.1.1. Motivation Elements

The motivation elements are a set of concepts used to model the various aspects of motivation and the forces that drive and influence an organization. These elements provide a structured approach to understanding, analyzing, and aligning an organization's motivations, goals, and objectives. By considering these elements, Enterprise Architects can effectively align the architecture with the strategic vision, manage change, and deliver value to stakeholders and the organization as a whole.

Table 6-1. *Motivation elements*

Element	Notation	
Stakeholder	Stakeholder	
Driver	Driver	
Goal	Goal	
Principle	Principle	!
Requirement	Requirement	

Stakeholder: Represents individuals, groups, or organizations that have an interest in the outcome of the architecture effort. Understanding stakeholders and their concerns is critical to aligning the architecture with their needs and expectations.

Driver: Represents the external or internal factors that create the need for change within the organization. These can be regulatory changes, market trends, business opportunities, or internal goals and strategies that drive architecture initiatives.

Goal: Is the desired result an organization wants to achieve. Goals represent the specific goals or objectives that the architecture must support. They help align the architecture with the strategic vision of the organization.

Objective: More specific than goals, objectives provide concrete, measurable targets that contribute to achieving the overall goals. Objectives help break high-level goals down into manageable and achievable components.

Principle: Is a basic guideline or rule that guides the Enterprise Architecture decision-making process. Principles help ensure consistency, promote best practices, and align architectural decisions with the organization's values and strategic goals.

Requirement: Describes the capabilities, features, or qualities that the architecture must have in order to meet the goals. Understanding requirements ensures that the architecture meets the needs of stakeholders and aligns with the organization's strategic intent.

Most of the motivation elements are described in Chapter 8. The stakeholder concept is explained in more detail in Section 8.2.2. Drivers, goals, objectives, and initiatives are discussed in Sections 8.3.3.1 through 8.3.3.4. Some of these elements also appear in Section 8.4.1. The development of basic principles and requirements, both part of the Framework Pyramid (Figure 8-15), is discussed further in Sections 8.3.2.2 and in 8.3.2.3.

6.2.1.2. Strategy Layer

The strategy layer allows one to model strategic aspects within the existing layers of Enterprise Architecture. It provides elements for modeling these strategic aspects to comprehensively capture and manage an organization's strategic initiatives and goals within the broader context of Enterprise Architecture.

Much like the motivation elements, the strategy layer elements allow Enterprise Architects to model how various architectural components (e.g., business processes, applications, technology infrastructure) align with and support the organization's strategic goals and objectives. They help communicate and visualize this alignment to stakeholders, ensuring that everyone understands how architectural decisions contribute to the broader goals. The elements provide decision-makers with a structured view of the organization's strategic landscape, enabling more informed decisions about architecture investments and changes.

Table 6-2. *Strategy layer elements*

Element	Notation	
Resource	Resource	
Capability	Capability	

Resource: Is often a critical component of an organization's asset management strategy. Resources are used for modeling and managing the various assets, materials, and elements that contribute to an organization's value creation and operational efficiency. By modeling resources, enterprise architects can gain insights into resource utilization, cost management, risk assessment, and alignment with strategic goals.

Capability: Are elements that can be employed to represent an organization's high-level abilities or competencies. These can include core business capabilities that are essential for executing the organization's strategy.

The strategy layer elements are featured in Chapter 8, Section 8.4.2, and in Chapter 10, Section 10.2.

6.2.1.3. Business Layer

The business layer focuses on modeling the business aspects of an organization, including its organizational structure, business processes, products, services, and the relationships among them.

The business layer elements provide a systematic and structured way to represent the business aspects of an organization (Business Architecture). They are essential for understanding, analyzing, and designing the Business Architecture, enabling the Enterprise Architect to ensure that business processes, functions, and interactions are aligned with the organization's strategic goals and objectives.

Table 6-3. *Business layer elements*

Element	Notation	
Business actor	Business Actor	
Business role	Business Role	
Business process	Business Process	
Business function	Business Function	
Business object	Business Object	

Business actor: Represents an external or internal entity that plays a specific role in the business. Business actors can be individuals, teams, departments, or even other organizations that interact with the business. The concept of a business actor is used throughout the book, and in most cases is used to describe a department of an organization.

Business role: A business role represents a specific function or position that an individual or group can play within the organization. It defines the responsibilities and behaviors associated with that role.

Business process: Represents a set of coordinated activities and behaviors that are performed to achieve specific business goals. Business processes show the flow of work and the relationships between different activities.

Business function: Represents a specific unit of the enterprise that performs a specific type of work, typically representing the higher-level capabilities of the organization.

Business object: Represents the concepts or things of interest to the business. Business objects can be products, orders, customers, or any other relevant business entity.

The business layer elements are most prominently featured in Chapter 8, Sections 8.2.1.1 through 8.2.1.3. The concept of a business process is explored throughout Section 8.2.1, particularly in the *Document* stage of the Enterprise Architecture Implementation Wheel (Figure 8-1).

6.2.1.4. Information Layer

The information layer focuses on modeling the information concepts within an organization, including the relationships between them.

The information layer elements provide a structured approach to representing and managing an organization's information concepts, part of the Information Architecture. They are essential for understanding information concepts within the organization, enabling the Enterprise Architect to design effective Information Architectures and ensure information quality. The information layer plays a critical role in supporting decision-making and ensuring that information is effectively managed across the organization.

Table 6-4. Information layer elements

Element	Notation	
Information concept	Information Concept	

Information concept: Information is considered an intangible, conceptual representation of things that exist in the real world. Information concepts form the basis of the architectural elements that are used to make these intangibles explicit. Information concepts are used to model a *business*, not an *IT system*. Section 8.2.1.3 of Chapter 8 explains the information concept and sheds light on how it relates to the business object concept.

6.2.1.5. Application Layer

The application layer focuses on modeling the software applications that support business functions and processes. It provides a structured representation of the Application Architecture that enables the Enterprise Architect to understand and manage the applications and their interactions within the organization.

The application layer elements represent and manage the organization's application architecture. They are essential for understanding the capabilities, functionalities, and interactions of applications within the organization, enabling the Enterprise Architect to design effective application portfolios, promote integration, and support business operations. The application layer plays an important role in optimizing application development, ensuring application security, and delivering a seamless user experience within the context of the Enterprise Architecture.

Table 6-5. *Application layer elements*

Element	Notation
Application component	Application Component
Data object	Data Object

Application component: Represents a modular and self-contained piece of software that provides specific application functionality. Application components can be stand-alone software applications or smaller modules within a larger application. Chapter 8, Section 8.2.1.4, shows how to use application components when implementing an Enterprise Architecture.

Data object: Represents a single piece of data that is relevant to the business. Data objects can represent tangible things, such as customer records, or intangible concepts, such as business rules. Data objects are referenced several times throughout the book.

6.2.1.6. Technology Layer

The technology layer focuses on modeling the technology infrastructure and resources that support the applications, data, and information within an organization. It provides a structured representation of the technology architecture that enables the Enterprise Architect to understand and manage the technology components and their interactions within the organization.

The technology layer elements represent and manage the organization's Technology Architecture. They are essential for understanding the capabilities, functionalities, and interactions of technology assets within the enterprise, enabling the Enterprise Architect to design effective technology infrastructures, promote integration, and support business operations. The technology layer plays a critical role in optimizing the use of technology, ensuring technology security, and delivering reliable technology services within the context of the Enterprise Architecture.

Table 6-6. *Technology layer elements*

Element	Notation	
Device	Device	
System software	System Software	
Technology service	Technology Service	
Artifact	Artifact	

Device: A physical technology resource that can be used to run software applications. Devices include desktop computers, laptops, smartphones, tablets, and other physical computing devices.

System software: Represents the software that manages and controls technology resources. System software includes operating systems, device drivers, middleware, and other foundational software.

Technology service: A piece of technology functionality exposed through an application interface. Technology services provide the capabilities that can be used by applications or other technology components.

Artifact: Represents a piece of data or information used or produced by a technology component. Artifacts include files, databases, logs, and other types of digital data.

The technology layer elements are explained in more detail in Chapter 8, Section 8.2.1.5. Artifacts are an exception, as they are mentioned in Section 8.3.1.3.

6.2.1.7. Composite Elements

Composite elements are elements used to combine or aggregate other elements from different layers or aspects of the architecture. They are a valuable tool for simplifying complex relationships and structures within the Enterprise Architecture. These composite elements allow architects to represent dynamic behavior, manage dependencies, and create organized and visually clear models. They help create more concise and coherent models by grouping related elements together. The composite element *location* is a bit of an oddity because the element has nothing to do with grouping elements.

Table 6-7. *Composite elements*

Element	Notation	
Location	Location	

Location: A location represents a conceptual or physical place or position where concepts are located or performed. The element is used to model the places where business actors, application components, and devices are located. In Chapter 8, Section 8.2.1.4, the location element is used to illustrate its application in relation to cloud services vs. on-premises services.

6.2.1.8. Implementation and Migration Layer

The implementation and migration layer is often used for comprehensive planning and execution of implementation and migration projects within the context of Enterprise Architecture.

The implementation and migration layer elements support the implementation and migration of architectures. This includes modeling implementation programs and projects to support program, portfolio, and project management. It also includes support for migration planning.

Table 6-8. *Implementation and migration layer elements*

Element	Notation	
Work package (initiative)	Work Package	
Deliverable	Deliverable	

Work package (initiative): A work package is typically not a continuous activity, but has a beginning and an end. It produces a well-defined set of results, typically modeled as deliverables. The work package element can be used to model entire projects or tasks within a project, programs, or project portfolios. In an Agile context, a work package can be used to model the work performed in an Agile iteration (e.g., sprint) or higher-level increment. Initiatives are very similar to work packages. Therefore, they share the same element.

Deliverable: Is an element produced by a work package. A deliverable can be any type of result. For example, reports, papers, services, software, physical products, etc., or intangible results such as organizational changes. A deliverable can also be the implementation of (part of) an architecture.

The implementation and migration layer element work package is featured in Chapter 8, Section 8.4.2. Deliverables are used for illustration purposes only in Appendix C: Example Work Package View.

ArchiMate provides a large number of architectural elements. This book names and describes only those elements that are used in the book. A complete overview of all elements can be found on The Open Group's website and in the book *ArchiMate 3.2 Specification* [12].

6.3. Catalogs, Matrices, and Diagrams

There is a lot going on in an organization, especially when a strategy is being implemented. This means that key players (stakeholders) within the organization may have questions or concerns about certain matters. For example, concerns that arise at the start of a project or program. Stakeholders may also have questions related to translating strategy into implementation, or they may have seemingly simpler concerns related to a specific application.

Typical questions or concerns stakeholders may have include

- What impact will this project have on day-to-day operations?

- What processes will be affected by this project?

- How does the implementation of certain initiatives relate to the execution of the strategy?

- Does the application support all the functionality that is needed?

The things that keep the stakeholders up at night and the questions they have are called *concerns*, and they need to be addressed. To answer them from an architecture perspective, catalogs, matrices, and diagrams are used. These architecture deliverables, as they are called, are standardized architecture products for capturing and visualizing information. This book regularly refers to a catalog, matrix, diagram, or map in the various chapters.

Catalogs: These are lists of building blocks of a specific type or related types that are used for governance or reference purposes (e.g., an organizational chart with locations and actors). A catalog addresses a specific concept (e.g., processes, applications, technology components) and supplements the information about the concept with additional data. It does not link to other concepts.

Table 6-9. *Example of a catalog*

Concept name	Value A	Value B
Concept A	...	...
Concept B	...	...
Concept C	...	...

Matrices: A matrix is a grid that represents the relationships between two or more model entities. The relationship between two or more concepts – typically spread across two or more catalogs – is brought together in a matrix.

Table 6-10. *Example of a matrix*

	Concept B		
	Concept B Value A	Concept B Value B	Concept B Value C
Concept A			
Concept A Value A	X		
Concept A Value B		X	
Concept A Value C			X

Diagrams (or maps): These are representations of architectural content in either graphical format (diagrams) or textual format (maps). Diagrams and maps can also be used as a technique for graphically populating architectural content or for verifying the completeness of collected information. The TOGAF Standard defines a set of architecture deliverables in the Content Framework (see Chapter 2, Figure 2-1). A diagram or map visualizes information captured in, for example, a catalog or matrix.

Table 6-11. *Example of a map*

Concept A (actor)	Concept B (process)	Concept C (service)
Actor A	Process A	Service A
Actor B	Process B	Service B
Actor C	Process C	Service C

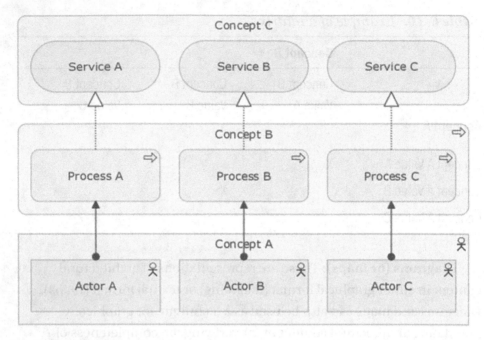

Figure 6-3. *Example of a diagram*

Knowing what can be captured and visualized is important for communicating with organizational stakeholders. As a general rule, less is more. Try to limit the amount of information in a catalog, matrix, diagram, or map. It is better to create more overviews than to overload existing overviews with information at the expense of the readability (and thus usability) of the architecture deliverables.

6.4. The Right Toolset

In order to feed the multitude of catalogs, matrices, and diagrams, with information about the organization, it is necessary to capture information about the organization's processes and information concepts. This also applies to the applications and technology objects. In a small organization, it may initially seem possible to use tools such as a word processor or presentation software (or even a spreadsheet application) to do this. However, it will soon become apparent that these (in themselves excellent) products do not provide the capabilities that an architect would want or need.

Consider, for example, the ability to change a relationship between two architectural elements. The change would then be automatically implemented in all models and diagrams that use that relationship. This could be a relationship between a server system and an application, or the relationship between a business actor (such as a business unit in the organization) and a business process. When using tools such as an *office suite* (or a similar product), any document, model, or diagram that contains the relationship just described must be modified the moment that relationship changes. So if a server system starts supporting a different application, or if a business unit is made responsible for a different process, changes would need to be made to all the documents that contain that particular relationship. Having a tool that allows you to make these types of changes with a single modification is indispensable when performing architecture work.

Another important feature is the ability to create elements with additional properties. As an example, consider the goal element (see Section 6.2.1.1). Creating an object representing a goal can, of course, be done in a tool such as Visio. But where architecture tools differ from the usual office products is that they can add all sorts of additional properties to such an element. Think, for example, of relationships to other elements (drivers, principles, requirements, and capabilities), or of plotting the element on a roadmap and supplementing it with initiatives (work packages). In some situations, adding user-created properties (such as cost or a responsible business role or unit) is a must. Architecture tools also provide additional visual insight into the progress of goal realization. By adding metrics as a property to the goal element, a goal can be made measurable. Spider charts (see Chapter 8, Section 8.5.1.1) graphically represent this.

These are just a few of the many examples that can be given to support the decision to use an architecture tool instead of the standard office products. Tools designed to capture architecture concepts and models often provide much more additional functionality than an average office product. Dedicated architecture tools make the life of an Enterprise Architect easier.

There are several architecture tools available on the market. Each tool has its own advantages and disadvantages. Gartner published its findings in a recent study on Enterprise Architecture tools [13]. Figure 6-3 shows which software vendors are significant players in the architecture tools market. Note that the vendors in the upper right quadrant are market leaders in specialized architecture software.

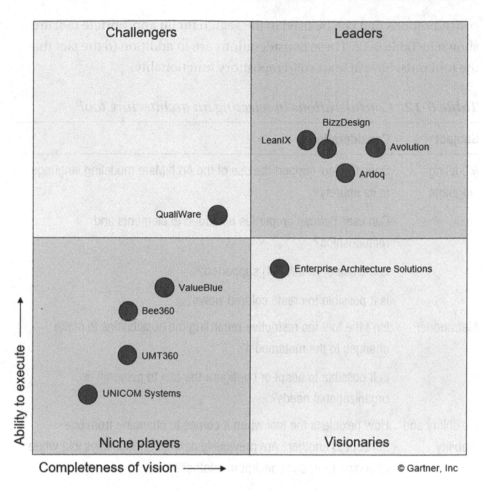

Figure 6-4. *Gartner Magic Quadrant – Enterprise Architecture tools (September 2022)*

Deciding which tool is best suited to use in the organization depends on several factors. Money, for example, is one such important factor. If there is a substantial budget available for Enterprise Architecture, it is easy to choose a tool in the Leaders quadrant (upper right). Tools in this quadrant generally have a slightly higher price tag than tools in the two lower quadrants. Therefore, if less money is available, the organization is more likely to choose a tool that is in one of the two lower quadrants. Some considerations that can be used in the search for an appropriate tool are shown in Table 6-12. These considerations are in addition to the fact that the tool must have at least solid repository functionality.

Table 6-12. *Considerations in selecting an architecture tool*

Subject	Consideration
Modeling language	Does the tool support the use of the ArchiMate modeling language in its entirety?
	Can user-defined properties be added to elements and relationships?
	Is the use of BPMN [14] supported?
	Is it possible to create colored views?
Metamodel	Isn't the tool too restrictive regarding the possibilities to make changes to the metamodel?
	Is it possible to adapt or configure the tool to personal or organizational needs?
Flexibility and stability	How flexible is the tool when it comes to changing from one concept to another? Are previously defined relationships lost when changing from one concept to another?
	How stable is the tool when editing or creating large and bulky models?
Import/export	Does the tool have import/export capabilities?
	Can the tool make information available to third parties who do not work with the tool?
	Can (large) PDF files be published for use as posters?
Support	Is the tool supported by a good help desk and user community?

The factors that ultimately determine the choice of an architecture tool depend on the situation. The same goes for the requirements for using a tool. These requirements are not easy to articulate – there is no standard set of requirements – because they are different for everyone.

6.4.1. Architecture Repository

The architecture tool selection described in Section 6.4 should, at a minimum, result in a product that can be used to build and maintain an Architecture Repository. Such an architecture repository consists of a collection of information about the organization's *Enterprise Architecture landscape,* a *reference library, standards,* and *requirements.*

A repository contains what is minimally needed to manage an Enterprise Architecture. Information that is not directly required for the Enterprise Architecture should not be included in the repository.

A well-managed repository is characterized by ruthlessly minimizing information collected and maintained [15].

6.4.1.1. Enterprise Architecture Landscape

The information about the Enterprise Architecture landscape consists of a collection of architecture products such as catalogs, matrices, diagrams, and maps. When using the Architecture Repository to provide projects or programs with the necessary visualizations and drawings, it is recommended to create a separate container for each individual project (see Figure 6-4). This way, the catalogs, matrices, diagrams, and maps needed for a specific project can be separated from other projects. This also applies to any reference materials or reference architectures, standards, and requirements.

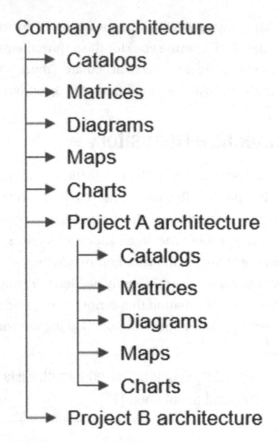

Figure 6-5. *Example of a repository structure*

Design the structure of the repository based on the architecture products and the needs of the organization. For example, this could be a hierarchical structure with folders and subfolders as shown in Figure 6-4. Make sure that the structure is intuitive and easy to navigate.

6.4.1.2. Reference Architecture

The Reference Library within the Architecture Repository provides all sorts of guidelines, templates, and other forms of reference material that can be used to speed up the process of creating an Enterprise Architecture.

For example, consider a reference architecture. Using a reference architecture can save a lot of time. Not everything needs to be inventoried and documented from scratch. The architect can focus on the differences between the reference model and the organization. What makes the organization unique from what is already captured in the reference architecture still needs to be inventoried and documented. There are often several models (business function model, information model, application function model, etc.) per industry that are part of a reference architecture. The use of a business function model, for example, ensures that the architect does not have to map every business function in the organization. Only the deviations and/or additions to the reference architecture need to be inventoried.

In addition to reference material in the form of models and architectures, there is a second type of reference material. This includes white papers, templates, and guides. The Series Guides that are part of the TOGAF Standard are a good example of documentary reference material. Figure 2-2 in Chapter 2, Section 2.3.1, shows how the Series Guides are organized and what information can be found in them. A complete list of available materials can be found on The Open Group's website.

6.4.1.3. Standards

Standards are also stored in the Architecture Repository. A standard can be defined at two different levels. One is the cross-organizational variant imposed by laws and regulations, and the other is the variant specified by the Enterprise Architecture.

Multi-factor authentication (MFA) is one example. Most organizations will need to adopt and implement some form of MFA. Certainly, hospitals and government agencies must meet stringent requirements for the security of the information they use and access. The use of MFA is mandated by laws and regulations. The final form of implementation is up to the institutions themselves, making it an Enterprise Architecture standard. A standard imposed by the Enterprise Architecture applies to all initiatives that use the architecture. Any initiative implemented under the banner of the architecture must take that standard into account.

Standards are derived from basic principles. The framework pyramid (see Figure 8-15 in Chapter 8, Section 8.3.2.1) shows this clearly. A basic principle such as *Comply with laws and regulations* supports the need to use the standard used in this example.

6.4.1.4. Requirements

The fourth and final minimum required component of the architecture repository is the subject of requirements. These requirements exist at different levels. If Enterprise Architecture is used in the organization to support the strategy (see Chapter 7), then the requirements will have a different profile than if Enterprise Architecture is required to provide support for the execution of the project portfolio. In the latter case, the requirements will relate to individual projects, on the one hand, and to the overall portfolio on the other. In the former case, where Enterprise Architecture is used to support the execution of the strategy, the requirements will manifest themselves more as derivatives of goals and objectives.

To arrive at an appropriate repository, it is important to focus on the intended use of the repository. The positioning of the architecture capability plays an important role in what the interpretation of the repository looks like. Understanding how the organization intends to practice Enterprise Architecture will help define the scope and required functionality. Regardless of where the architecture capability is located, the repository must be regularly updated and maintained. All new changes must be documented, and new architectural products must be added. It is equally important to remove obsolete or irrelevant products from the repository. The Architecture Repository must be kept up to date with the organization's changing Enterprise Architecture.

6.5. Summary

Chapter 6 focused on visualizing architecture.

- It showed why it is important to use a consistent and uniform language when communicating with the organization.

- It explained the role that a modeling language plays in visualizing architecture models and diagrams.

- The chapter also gave a glimpse into the origins of the modeling language.

- The architecture products (deliverables) catalog, matrix, diagram, and map were explained, and the importance of using a good architecture tool was emphasized.

- The need for an Architecture Repository, what it contains, and the reasons why products such as an office suite are inadequate were also addressed.

CHAPTER 7

Architecture Positioning

Chapter 7 looks at how architecture can be positioned in an organization. The four different ways described by the TOGAF Standard are each briefly explained, and the implications of each positioning are noted. Examples of architecture work appropriate to each positioning are also given.

7.1. Earning Stripes

The average organization that has little or no exposure to architecture will not immediately see the benefits of the structured approach that Enterprise Architecture has to offer. Despite the fact that such an organization has decided to hire an architect, it will not immediately see an Enterprise Architect as the go-to guy or girl. To dispel the illusion right away, no board of directors or management will see the added value of an Enterprise Architect out of the gate. Stripes have to be earned first.

Those stripes can be earned by establishing a solid basic Enterprise Architecture: a foundation that consists of captured information about the organization, the processes and information concepts in use, the applications, and the information systems. This information can then be made available to stakeholders in the form of catalogs, matrices, diagrams, and maps. It is essential to identify who the key stakeholders are and

© Eric Jager 2023
E. Jager, *Getting Started with Enterprise Architecture*,
https://doi.org/10.1007/978-1-4842-9858-9_7

what their concerns are. It is also important to determine how mature an organization is when it comes to working with architecture, and to have insight into what the strategic direction looks like.

Creating a basic Enterprise Architecture allows the architect to use the information gathered to confirm or disconfirm assumptions made during projects. It enables the architect to establish and deploy frameworks that allow the organization to gain traction and control over project and program initiatives. By applying architectural skills and capabilities, the architect is able to translate the organization's strategic direction into execution. Enterprise Architecture is thus a highly valuable tool for the organization. Getting this message across is critical to the continued growth of architecture skills and capabilities within the organization.

7.2. Architecture Purpose

Unfortunately, it is not always possible to establish an Enterprise Architecture in its most mature form. Much depends on the organization's view of the use of the architecture capability. The TOGAF Standard describes four ways in which an architecture capability is typically used [16]. Figure 7-1 shows schematically the four possible implementations of the architecture capability.

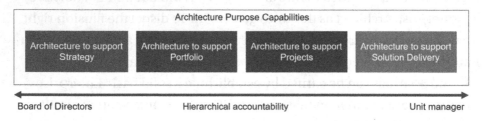

Figure 7-1. *Enterprise Architecture Capability model*

In support of strategy: Enterprise Architecture is used to develop a target architecture and create roadmaps that reflect organizational changes within the enterprise over a three- to ten-year period.

In this context, Enterprise Architecture is used to support enterprise-wide change requests and multiple projects and programs, and to achieve strategy execution through these projects and programs. There is ample room for Enterprise Architecture to shape strategic aspects such as drivers, goals, objectives, and initiatives. Enterprise Architecture used to support strategy is architecture in its most comprehensive form.

In support of portfolio: Enterprise Architecture supports change initiatives that span multiple functions, phases, and projects.

An architecture for this purpose will primarily focus on a single portfolio. An example of a single portfolio might be migrating to a cloud environment. Within the portfolio, which has a clearly defined scope, multiple projects will require the support of Enterprise Architecture. In this context, architecture is used to interpret and guide projects. The architect ensures the alignment of the projects within the portfolio, the coherence of the projects, and steers their execution. Enterprise Architecture is thus less of an organizational steering function than when it is primarily concerned with strategy execution.

In support of projects: The use of Enterprise Architecture is tailored to the project delivery method of the organization.

An architecture for this purpose typically covers one project. To stay in the context of migrating to a cloud environment, consider moving an on-premises customer relationship management system to its counterpart in a cloud environment. This migration requires the architect's involvement not only in the Application Architecture domain, but certainly in the Business and Information Architecture domains as well. In the context of supporting projects, Enterprise Architecture is used to clarify the purpose and value of the project, as well as to identify requirements and monitor adherence to architecture governance. In addition, architecture supports integration and alignment across projects.

In support of solution delivery: Enterprise Architecture supports the delivery of solutions.

An architecture used for this purpose typically covers one project or a significant portion of a project. The architecture is used to define how the change will be designed and delivered, and to identify constraints, controls, and architectural requirements for the design. The architecture provides a governance framework for the change. Enterprise Architecture used to support solution delivery is actually similar to Solution Architecture. If the organization chooses this use of architecture, the question arises as to whether the organization would benefit more from employing a Solution Architect than an Enterprise Architect.

It is important to find out how the organization views and interprets the architecture capability. What are the organization's desires and requirements regarding the architecture capability? The position of the architecture capability in the organization gives an indication of how it is viewed. The higher the direct reporting line is in the organizational hierarchy, the more the architecture capability moves toward the strategic side of the discipline. Figure 7-2 provides some insight into the possible placement of the architecture capability within the organization.

For example, if an Enterprise Architect reports directly to the CEO of an organization, then the deployment of the architecture capability will be primarily in the strategic domain. If the direct reporting line is to the CIO, then the architect is more likely to be involved in portfolio and project management. If the direct reporting line is to the unit manager of an IT department, then the architecture role includes the solution delivery side of the architecture capability.

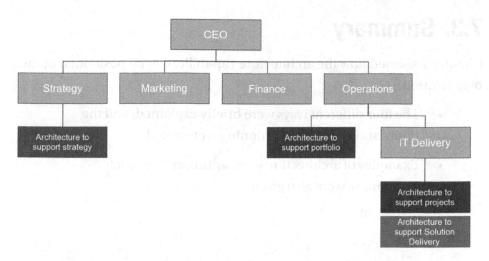

Figure 7-2. *Positioning of the architecture capability*

Chapter 8, Section 8.2.1.1, discusses the creation of a Business Roles Map. This map clarifies how roles are distributed throughout the organization. A Business Roles Map can help locate the position of the architecture capability and reveals much about the organization's view of the interpretation of the architecture capability. The activities that the Enterprise Architect will perform once the foundation has been laid depend largely on the chosen interpretation of the architecture function.

Please note that there is no right or wrong way to use the architecture capability. The position of the architecture capability primarily influences the focus areas of the Enterprise Architect and the associated initiatives and activities.

7.3. Summary

Chapter 7 showed how the architecture capability can be positioned in the organization.

- The four different ways were briefly explained, and the implications of each positioning were noted.

- Examples of architecture work appropriate to each positioning were also given.

CHAPTER 8

Architecture Implementation

Chapter 8 describes the actual implementation of a basic Enterprise Architecture. Guided by the Enterprise Architecture Implementation Wheel and using clearly defined architecture products (deliverables), each domain of the Enterprise Architecture is mapped out. Each of the stages defined in the Enterprise Architecture Implementation Wheel is covered in detail. The stages of documenting, defining, implementing, and monitoring are discussed step by step. Through personal experience, examples, and detailed explanations, the book works toward the implementation of a basic Enterprise Architecture.

8.1. Implementation Wheel

The complexity of the field of architecture has been discussed in the previous chapters. The origins of architecture, the various architecture domains and roles, as well as the many different definitions that exist have been explained. Now, it is time to take a step-by-step approach to implementing Enterprise Architecture. The sequence of steps described in this book is based on experience gained over the years with a wide range of employers, large and small, and in a variety of industries.

© Eric Jager 2023
E. Jager, *Getting Started with Enterprise Architecture,*
https://doi.org/10.1007/978-1-4842-9858-9_8

The use of architecture frameworks helps an architect to determine the steps of the topics that need to be covered to establish an Enterprise Architecture. However, the sequence of certain steps described in architecture frameworks may not always be implemented in that specific order in practice.

In particular, it is this sequence that manifests itself differently in practice than in theory. The first phases described in an architecture framework involve setting and articulating goals and objectives. Practice shows, however, that when an Enterprise Architect starts a new job in an existing organization, many of these goals have already been determined. After all, it is safe to assume that the organization has been in existence for more than a few weeks or months. Of course, this is a bit different for a start-up or scale-up organization. Such an organization has not been in existence for very long, and it is likely that a start-up or scale-up organization would benefit from hiring an Enterprise Architect to help formulate the strategy and associated goals and objectives.

An existing organization – and the form can vary greatly – often has a draft strategic direction consisting of drivers, goals, objectives, and intended outcomes. Not in every situation will these three elements be equally well and comprehensively described, but most likely they will not be missing.

With these experiences in mind, I have tried to provide a roadmap for implementing Enterprise Architecture in an existing organization.

I realize that there are additional areas and topics of interest when we talk about a complete Enterprise Architecture.

However, the focus of this book is on the initial implementation of Enterprise Architecture in an existing organization, and therefore does not describe the full content of an average architecture framework.

It is about providing tools that can help in establishing an Enterprise Architecture.

To reinforce the process of implementing Enterprise Architecture in an existing organization, a self-created Enterprise Architecture Implementation Wheel was developed (see Figure 8-1). The Implementation Wheel is a combined visualization of the steps taken in different organizations. The steps themselves, as well as the order of the steps, are based on experience gained over the years. The wheel should be read clockwise, starting from the inside out.

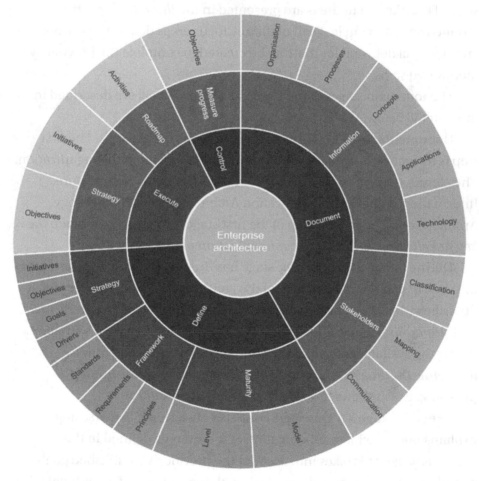

Figure 8-1. *Enterprise Architecture Implementation Wheel*

The Enterprise Architecture Implementation Wheel is built around the *central circle*, Enterprise Architecture.

The *first ring* around the center is the ring that defines the four main stages of the Implementation Wheel. Each stage consists of one or more steps. The steps form the *second ring* around the center circle and provide valuable information on how to approach each stage. The steps also define a number of key focus areas that are relevant to these steps. These key focus areas are presented in the *third and final ring* around the center circle. Each of the key focus areas details the various architectural deliverables that can be created to complete the previously mentioned steps.

The four main stages of the Implementation Wheel are described in more detail below.

Document (stage 1): This first stage consists of two steps. The first step is to *capture and document the elements of interest* to the organization. The elements are in all architecture domains (Business Architecture, Information Architecture, Application Architecture, and Technology Architecture). The second step of the first stage is to *classify and map the key stakeholders* and *create a communication plan*.

Define (stage 2): The *Define* stage has three steps. First, it determines the *current and desired maturity* of the architecture capability. Second, it describes what is involved in *establishing basic principles, requirements, and standards*. Finally, it focuses on defining the organization's strategy (using the available information). Guidance is provided on how to *determine the drivers, goals,* and *objectives* that the organization is pursuing. It also shows how to identify related *initiatives*.

Execute (stage 3): This stage consists of two steps. The first step explains how to achieve an execution of the strategy defined in the previous stage. This takes into account the previously established goals and objectives. The second step deals with the creation of a roadmap based on the objectives to be achieved and the related initiatives and activities.

Control (stage 4): The final stage, *Control*, is concerned with measuring the progress of the implementation of a basic Enterprise Architecture. It also explains how to visualize the progress of the realization of the organizational goals and objectives. The initiatives and activities to be carried out are monitored and made measurable. To this end, it discusses a number of measurement tools and techniques that can be used to visualize progress.

The stages in the Implementation Wheel consist of steps. The level of detail increases as the Implementation Wheel is read from the inside out. The above stages and associated steps are based on and inspired by the TOGAF Standard. They can therefore be mapped to the phases of the Architecture Development Method (ADM) [17]. Table 8-1 shows the relationship between the Implementation Wheel stages on the one hand and the ADM stages on the other. The phases of the ADM listed in Table 8-1 are explained in more detail in Chapter 2, Section 2.3.1.1.

Table 8-1. *Stages of the Enterprise Architecture Implementation Wheel*

Stage of Implementation Wheel	Step	Focus area	TOGAF ADM phase
Document	Information	Organization	Phase B
		Processes	Phase B
		Concepts	Phase C
		Applications	Phase C
		Technology	Phase D
	Stakeholders	Classification	Phase A
		Mapping	Phase A
		Communication	Phase A

(*continued*)

Table 8-1. (*continued*)

Stage of Implementation Wheel	Step	Focus area	TOGAF ADM phase
Define	Maturity	Model	Phase A
		Level	Phase A
	Framework	Principles	Preliminary Phase
		Requirements	Phase B, C, D
		Standards	Phase B, C, D
	Strategy	Drivers	Preliminary Phase
		Goals	Preliminary Phase
		Objectives	Preliminary Phase
		Initiatives	Preliminary Phase
Execute	Strategy	Objectives	Phase F
		Initiatives	Phase F
	Roadmap	Activities	Phase E, F
Control	Measure progress	Objectives	Phase G, H

Going through the four stages of the Implementation Wheel can help build a solid basic Enterprise Architecture. This does not mean that each stage and its steps must be followed to the letter. Every organization is different, and some organizations or situations require a different way of working. The Implementation Wheel should therefore be seen primarily as a source of inspiration, but it can provide guidance at the start of an Enterprise Architecture implementation. The four stages of the Enterprise Architecture Implementation Wheel are further explained in Sections 8.2 through 8.5.

8.2. Document

The first stage of the Implementation Wheel is *Document*. This stage consists of two steps, *Information* and *Stakeholders*. The first step is to capture the key information needed to arrive at a basic Enterprise Architecture. This is done using the catalogs, matrices, diagrams, and maps described in Chapter 6, Section 6.3. The second step is to identify and understand the needs, interests, expectations (the stakeholder concerns), and communication preferences of the various stakeholders. Both steps are outlined in the following pages, along with a description for each of the key focus areas.

Table 8-2. First stage of the Enterprise Architecture Implementation Wheel

Document		Define			Execute		Control
Information	Stakeholders	Maturity	Framework	Strategy	Strategy	Roadmap	Measure progress

8.2.1. Information

In order to gather information about the organization, its organizational layout, hierarchical relationships, and any influencers, it is important to talk to people in the organization. Conducting one-on-one interviews often provides more information than what can be gleaned from the various documents that have been created to depict the organization. The same approach can be used to gather information about the processes and information used in the organization, as well as the applications and IT systems.

Now, it is an illusion to think that gathering the necessary information during an initial tour of the organization will be particularly successful. You will not get a 100% conclusive overview. Gathering information about how the organization works, what exactly goes on there, and what processes are used and executed takes time. The same goes for gaining insight into the applications and information systems in use. Fortunately, gaining a 100% conclusive view is not the goal of the first stage of the Implementation Wheel. What can be pursued is the 80/20 rule; get an 80% accurate view and leave the 20% for later. The 80% that is accurate provides enough input to start the conversation about the remaining 20% that is missing or incomplete.

If, at the end of the inventory period, it can be said that 80% of the processes have been mapped, a tremendous outcome has been realized. The remaining 20% will eventually follow. However, experience shows that in most cases, capturing the remaining 20% takes a multiple of the initial inventory time. Taking stock of an organization requires a careful approach, and that simply takes time. A lot of time. But in the context of Enterprise Architecture, quality always takes precedence over speed.

When gathering information, it helps a tremendous amount to talk to people in the organization. They are the ones who worked for the organization before the decision was made to get started with architecture. The employees are the ones who have the best view of how the organization works. What processes and information are performed and processed, and what applications and technologies are used to support those processes.

In this inventory stage, go with the organizational language and try to speak the language of the organization. The conversation about definitions can always come later. Are people talking about a process when, in the world of architecture, it should be a business function? If so, just call it a process in the conversations. Defining whether something is a business function or a process will follow eventually. At this point, it would only cause confusion. It may even make people less inclined to share the information you are seeking.

When starting to work with architecture in an organization where it is not sufficiently present or developed, the advice is to first lay out the groundwork. Make sure that this foundation consists of deliverables that cover all areas of the architecture. This will provide a basis to start the conversation with the people in the organization. This information base can be tested against the principles, requirements, and standards to be established later (see Section 8.3.2).

Table 8-3. *Deliverables of stage one – Document/Information*

Deliverable	Description
Organization Map	Visualizes the interaction (internal and external, with partners and suppliers) of the organization
Business Roles Map	Displays the governance structure of the company
Business Process Map	Listing of business processes in use, linked where possible to business functions and process owners
Business Function/Business Process Matrix	Cross-mapping of business functions and processes
Organization/Business Process Matrix	Cross-mapping of business units and processes
Information Map	Listing of information concepts in use
Information Concept/ Business Process Matrix	Cross-mapping of information concepts and processes
Application Portfolio Catalog	Listing of applications in use, both internal and external (e.g., cloud services purchased)
Application/Information Concept Matrix	Cross-mapping of applications and information concepts
Application/Business Process Matrix	Cross-mapping of applications and business processes
Technology Portfolio Catalog	Enumeration of (server) systems in use, both internal and external (e.g., technological cloud services)
Technology/Application Matrix	Cross-mapping of used (server) systems and applications
Technology/Application Function Map	Mapping technology functionality onto application functionality

Table 8-3 provides an overview of the architecture deliverables that should be created during the first stage of the Implementation Wheel. Use these architecture deliverables to capture the information you find, and store it in the Architecture Repository. Creating these deliverables provides a solid foundation for the Enterprise Architecture. This foundation can be built upon over time and supplemented with all sorts of catalogs, matrices, diagrams, and maps.

8.2.1.1. Organization

Table 8-4. Deliverables of the focus area Organization

Deliverable	Description
Organization Map	Visualizes the interaction (internal and external, with partners and suppliers) of the organization
Business Roles Map	Displays the governance structure of the company

Organization Map

The first focus of the information to be found is in the area of what the organization looks like in terms of internal and external interaction. It is interesting and necessary to take stock of what the organization looks like in terms of relationships between departments and boards, as well as between suppliers and partners. External parties often play a significant role as well. An Organization Map is used to visualize the internal and external relationships.

An Organization Map contains the key organizational units, partners, and stakeholder groups that make up the enterprise ecosystem. The map should also depict the working relationship between those entities, as distinct from an organizational chart that only shows hierarchical reporting relationships. The map is typically depicted as a network or web of relationships and interactions between the various business entities [18].

As the quote above indicates, the key is to map the organizational units (the business units or departments). Key stakeholders, suppliers, and partners should also be included in the overview.

Start by looking at the company's organizational chart. This often provides a good insight into the different departments or business units within the organization. Conversations can be held with these units to gather additional information. The Organization Map should show the relationships between the organizational units on the one hand and the stakeholders (internal and external) on the other. This is different from an organization chart, which only describes the internal hierarchical relationships. An Organization Map typically shows a web or network of relationships between the different business units (divisions or departments).

To arrive at an Organization Map, the following questions can be asked:

- Where is the unit or department located hierarchically in the organization where the work is performed?

- Does it collaborate with other departments or units within the organization?

- Does it collaborate with partners and suppliers?

The answers to these questions should provide a picture of the business unit's hierarchical position within the organization and its relationships with other internal units. They should also answer any partnerships with partners and suppliers.

An Organization Map is created by connecting the business units, partners, and suppliers to the organization itself. Start with the organization (shown in the center of Figure 8-2), and link the boards and business units to it. Then link the partners and suppliers to the appropriate organizational units. Have stakeholders test the model for accuracy.

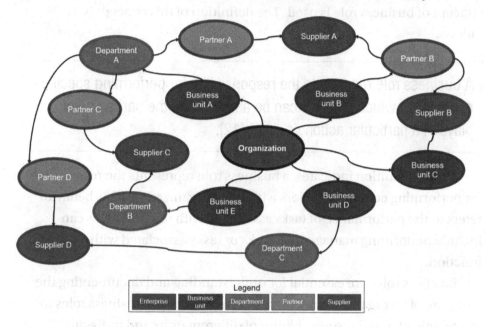

Figure 8-2. *Organization Map*

Capture the Organization Map in the Architecture Repository (see Chapter 6, Section 6.4.1) for later reuse. All of the architecture deliverables mentioned in this book should be captured in the repository.

Business Roles Map

Organizational structures are more than just a hierarchy. It is therefore useful to map not only the organizational structure but also the responsibilities of business units, departments, and other organizational actors. It is advisable not to limit the view to the usual and more formal actors; informal stakeholders can be just as influential as the formal ones.

The level of detail of this mapping can go down to the level of individual responsibilities, for example. In practice, knowledge of responsibilities is essential to any business, and therefore to Enterprise Architecture.

To define the different roles within an organization, the architecture concept of business role is used. The definition of this concept is as follows.

A business role represents the responsibility for performing specific behavior, to which an actor can be assigned, or the part an actor plays in a particular action or event [12].

As the definition indicates, a business role represents the responsibility for performing certain behaviors within the organization. This behavior refers to the performance of tasks associated with that role. This can include performing management tasks or tasks associated with a specific function.

Business roles are essential for understanding and documenting the structure of an organization. Enterprise Architects use business roles to model the roles and responsibilities of different units and individuals within the organization. This helps to analyze the organizational hierarchy and ensure that responsibilities are appropriately distributed.

When modeling business processes, business roles are used to define who is responsible for specific activities or tasks. By assigning business roles to process steps, architects can easily identify the actors involved in each activity and understand the flow of work within the organization. Business Roles help define responsibility and accountability within an organization. By assigning roles to specific tasks, it becomes clear who is responsible for the successful completion of each task, promoting better governance and decision-making.

Business roles are also associated with business capabilities. A capability represents what an organization is capable of doing. By mapping business roles to capabilities, the Enterprise Architect can determine which roles are essential to perform specific business functions. This analysis helps with workforce planning and identifying critical roles for successful business operations. The use of business roles help the Enterprise Architect to understand, analyze, and design the organizational structure, business processes, and capabilities within an organization. It provides a clear view of responsibilities and accountabilities, enabling better decision-making, effective governance, and alignment of business and IT strategies.

By using the business role concept, the governance structure of the organization can be visualized. For example, a business roles map can provide insight into the positioning of the architecture capability within the organization. A Business Roles Map goes beyond an organizational chart.

To capture the different roles within an organization, the following questions can be asked:

- Who reports to whom or is accountable for work done?

- Who is accountable for the work done?

- To whom does the business unit or department head report?

- What departments does the business unit consist of?

- What is the hierarchy of the department or unit?

- Are there additional roles that someone in the business unit or department performs?

Gaining an understanding of the different roles that exist within the organization helps to create a Business Roles Map. The answers to these questions can be used to create a more detailed map than, for example, an organizational chart.

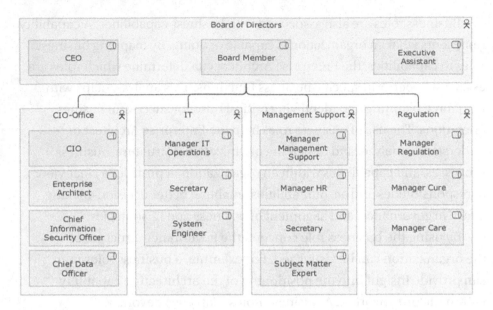

Figure 8-3. *Business Roles Map*

When visualizing business roles, try to keep the diagram or map clean. Sometimes this means that business roles that do not play a significant role in the overall picture are better left out. However, it is desirable to include all the roles in the created model – even the omitted ones – in the Architecture Repository.

8.2.1.2. Processes

Table 8-5. *Deliverables of the focus area Processes*

Deliverable	Description
Business Process Map	Listing of business processes in use, linked to business functions and process owners
Business Function/Business Process Matrix	Cross-mapping of business functions and processes
Organization/Business Process Matrix	Cross-mapping of business units and processes

A business process plays a critical role in analyzing, optimizing, and aligning an organization's operations with its strategic goals. By understanding and modeling business processes, the Enterprise Architect can design effective business solutions, streamline operations, and ensure that technology and business strategies are tightly integrated for overall business success. A business process represents a set of related activities or tasks performed by an organization to achieve a specific business goal or produce a specific output. Business processes are fundamental to the functioning of an organization because they define how work is performed and how different parts of the organization work together to deliver products or services.

Enterprise architects use process modeling techniques to identify bottlenecks, redundancies, and areas for improvement, enabling them to optimize business processes for better performance and resource utilization. They also serve as the foundation for workflow automation initiatives. By modeling and understanding the sequence of tasks and activities, architects can identify opportunities for automation and implement technology solutions that streamline and accelerate business operations. By identifying opportunities for significant process redesign and reengineering, this can lead to radical improvements in business efficiency, cost reduction, and customer satisfaction.

Business processes are essential to ensure compliance with regulations and internal governance policies. By modeling processes, architects can identify areas of non-compliance and design controls to ensure compliance.

Finally, business processes serve as a bridge between business and IT. Architects can analyze processes to understand the IT systems and applications that support them, ensuring that technology solutions are aligned with the operational needs of the business. During business transformations or major changes in the organization, understanding business processes helps architects assess the impact of these changes. They can then develop plans to transition from the current state to the future state with minimal disruption.

Business Process Map

A Business Process Map is essentially an overview of all the processes used by an organization. These processes are (detailed) descriptions of the steps an employee takes or a system performs that ultimately lead to an end product or service.

An average organization may know and use up to hundreds of processes. Mapping them all can be a daunting task. Creating a coherent Business Process Map is therefore a difficult task for an Enterprise Architect. It requires a lot of research and countless conversations with people in an organization to correctly map all the processes used.

What can help in creating a first draft of the Business Process Map is to inventory not the processes, but the business functions. Business functions are a collection or cluster of business processes.

The definitions of a business function and a business process are as follows.

A business function represents a collection of business behavior based on a chosen set of criteria such as required business resources and/or competencies, and is managed or performed as a whole [12].

A business process represents a sequence of business behaviors that achieves a specific result such as a defined set of products or business services [12].

A business function is a *collection* of behaviors, as opposed to a business process, which is a *sequence* of behaviors.

To document business processes, start by gathering information that is readily available, such as the organization's intranet pages. Most organizations have an intranet, and it is often filled with valuable information about existing departments and their activities. The activities of departments are often described in detail, and there is more than enough information about what a department claims to do or what it can be used for.

Therefore, this information should be collected directly and translated into business functions. For example, if a department states that it performs analysis on data, this immediately leads to the business function Analyze Data. If it is stated somewhere that a department is involved in publishing documents on the corporate website or elsewhere, then the business function Publish Information or Publish Public Information can be extracted. A department such as Legal Affairs is often concerned with providing legal support, and Human Resources as a department is undoubtedly concerned with recruiting, onboarding, and maintaining personnel records.

Once there is an understanding of the business functions used, the conversation can begin with the relevant departments to find out what activities are performed within the context of the business functions found. This leads to the capture of business processes.

Within each department, ask the following questions to identify the processes used:

- What actions are performed during work?
- Are these actions in an application or are they process actions?
- Is someone in the department responsible for these actions?
- The business function [name] is related to the department. How is it performed?

Record all the described processes and actions in the Architecture Repository. Then compare the described operations, and remove any duplication. If possible, add the process owner directly.

Table 8-6. *Business Process Map*

Process name	Process owner	Business function
Process A	Business unit/role A	Business function A
Process B	Business unit/role B	Business function A
Process C	Business unit/role C	Business function A
Process D	Business unit/role A	Business function B
Process E	Business unit/role D	Business function B
Process F	Business unit/role D	Business function C

A Business Process Map can also be represented graphically using a Business Process Diagram. Both the map and the diagram provide insight into which processes belong to which business functions, and thus form the basis for the next deliverable to be created.

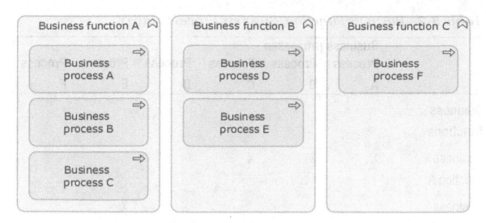

Figure 8-4. *Business Process Diagram*

Business Function/Business Process Matrix

Once a Business Process Map is in place, listing and describing all the processes used in the organization, it can be combined with other elements to gain additional insight. By cross-mapping the processes from the Business Process Map to the business functions captured, the relationship between the business functions and the business processes can be visualized. A cross-mapping is a relationship between two variables that shows the cause-and-effect relationship between them. From a Business Function/Business Process Matrix, it is easy to see where there is overlap in the use of processes. Ideally, a business process should not be used in more than one business function. Processes that do appear in multiple business functions may need to be reviewed. These overlapping processes may not be described with sufficient clarity or detail so that they appear to belong to multiple business functions.

In summary, a business function can consist of multiple business processes, but none of these processes should be part of multiple business functions. Of course, it is possible for a process in a given business function to call another process. In this case, the called process may be in a different business function.

Table 8-7. *Business Function/Business Process Matrix*

| | Business processes | | | | | |
	Process A	Process B	Process C	Process D	Process E	Process F
Business functions						
Business function A	X	X	X			
Business function B				X	X	
Business function C						X

The Business Function/Business Process Matrix should be used primarily to provide an insight into overlapping processes. It is these processes that should be brought to light.

An example of overlapping processes is shown in Figure 8-5. The situation is that of an organization that sells products to customers. Customers can order products, after which the product is packaged, an invoice is prepared, and the product is shipped. In parallel, payment for the order is processed, and customer information is updated with the order information.

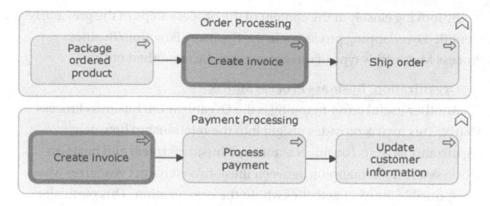

Figure 8-5. *Example of overlapping processes*

In the example (Figure 8-5), the *Create Invoice* process appears to exist in both the *Order Processing* and *Payment Processing* business functions. In reality, after the order is packed, the Payment Processing business function is triggered (see Figure 8-6), and the Create Invoice process is called. It is the Payment Processing business function that actually contains the Create Invoice process. Creating an invoice is more logically located in the second business function than in the first. This is because the first business function is about *handling an ordered product*, while the second is about *handling it administratively*.

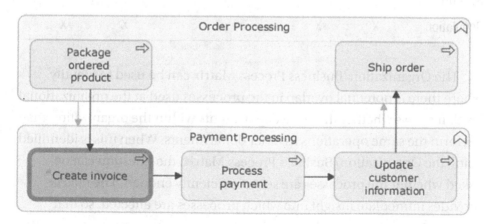

Figure 8-6. *Example of an invoked process*

By looking closely at the content of the process steps of the previously identified overlapping processes in the Business Function/Business Process Matrix, this type of unevenness can be smoothed out.

Organization/Business Process Matrix

Another useful cross-mapping is the Organization/Business Process Matrix. This matrix provides insight into the relationship between organizational units (business actors and business roles) and business processes. A cross-mapping between these two elements visualizes who is responsible for what activities within the organization. This particular cross-mapping is called an Organization/Business Process Matrix.

Table 8-8. *Organization/Business Process Matrix*

	Business processes					
	Process A	Process B	Process C	Process D	Process E	Process F
Business units						
CIO Office			X		X	
IT	X		X	X		
Management Support		X		X		X
Regulation	X	X			X	X

The Organization/Business Process Matrix can be used to identify where there is potential overlap in the processes used at the organizational level. It shows whether there are departments within the organization that perform the same operations as other departments. When this is identified using the Organization/Business Process Matrix, the question can be asked whether the processes are set up efficiently enough. The matrix provides immediate insight into which processes are affected, so that targeted improvement actions can be taken.

8.2.1.3. Concepts

Table 8-9. *Deliverables of the focus area Concepts*

Deliverable	Description
Information Map	Listing of information concepts in use
Information Concept/Business Process Matrix	Cross-mapping of information concepts and processes

Information Map

The Information Map is a schematic representation of the set of *information concepts* and their interrelationships that are important to an organization. Information is considered an intangible, conceptual representation of things that exist in the real world. Information concepts form the basis of the architectural elements that are used to make these intangibles explicit. Information concepts are used to model a *business*, not an *IT system*.

Information concepts reflect the language spoken within the organization (the corporate vocabulary, such as customer, account, or product). The great advantage of having an Information Map is the ability to communicate unambiguously within the organization and across departments, using a consistent and uniform language that is known within the organization.

A completed Information Map provides insight into the issues that are important to the organization and allows the architect to determine where this information will be used.

The Information Map of a business is most useful when cross-mapped to the capabilities, strategic plans, and initiatives that require changes in how information is employed by the business [19].

In addition to the definition shown, an information concept can also be related to business processes and applications.

The TOGAF Standard explains the concept of Information Mapping in the Series Guide: Information Mapping [20] and bases the creation of an Information Map on the content as described in the BIZBOK Guide [19].

Identifying the information concepts to be included in the Information Map begins with identifying the elements that are most important to the business. One way to get an overview of the existing information concepts is to listen to the nouns used when people talk about different topics within the organization. Every noun is potentially an information concept. By distilling the nouns from the conversations, it is possible to determine whether they represent an information item that the organization values.

This sounds like a difficult task, but in practice it is not difficult at all. Listen carefully to the conversations and note the nouns being used. Keep a list and remove duplicate or similar words. In this way, an 80% conclusive list of topics of interest to the organization – information concepts – can be produced fairly quickly.

Another source of information concepts is the laws and regulations that apply to the organization.

For example, I once worked for an organization that was required by law to create regulations, tariffs, and policies.

I included these last three nouns in the Information Map because they are important information concepts for the company.

Ask the following questions to identify key information concepts:

- What are the organization's key deliverables?

- What products and services does the organization provide to customers?

- What types of information are used?

- Looking at key processes, what laws and regulations govern them?
- Do applicable laws and regulations require the creation of specific products and services?

A spreadsheet tool can be used initially to capture information concepts. As this is done, be sure to collect and record as much additional information as possible so that cross-mappings can be made later. When recording additional information, consider determining the category of the information concept and its relationship to other information concepts. A clear definition of the information concept should also be included. Because the list will need to be added to frequently, especially at the beginning, it is faster and more efficient to use a spreadsheet tool than the Architecture Repository. In the end, all information concepts should be registered in the repository along with the Information Map.

Table 8-10. *Information Map*

Information concept	Information concept category	Information concept definition	Related information concepts
Strategy	Primary	An integrated pattern and perspective that aligns an organization's goals, objectives, and action sequences into a cohesive whole	Goal, Objective
Goal	Secondary	An end toward which effort is or should be directed	Objective
Objective	Secondary	A quantitative, measurable result that defines strategy	Initiative
Initiative	Secondary	A coordinated collection of temporary endeavors undertaken to create a unique outcome	Strategy

At a minimum, the following columns should be used when creating an Information Map.

Information concept: The Information Map names and contains all the information concepts that exist and are important in the organization. The information concept realizes a business object, where the business object defines the basic naming convention for the information concept.

Information concept category: There are two categories of information concepts. A *primary* information concept realizes a business object that is not dependent on another business object. A *secondary* information concept realizes a business object that is dependent on another business object. For example, the information concept Strategy is a primary information concept. It exists on its own and does not depend on any other business object. Information concepts such as Goal, Objective, and Initiative are secondary information concepts because they depend on a business object (in this case, the Strategy business object).

Information concept definition: The definition of an information concept is derived from the (business) object part of the capability definition and omits the action part of the definition. For example, if the capability is called Strategy Management, the business object would be called Strategy, which would also be the name for the information concept.

Related information concepts: Relationships between information concepts mirror relationships between business objects. In many cases, related information concepts are a logical derivative of the primary information concept. For example, Goal and Objective are both direct derivatives of Strategy. Initiative, on the other hand, is an indirect derivative of Strategy and can exist without the presence of Strategy because it also has a relationship with, for example, the Portfolio information concept. Therefore, for the primary information concept Strategy, the secondary information concepts Goal, Objective, and Initiative are listed in the related information concepts column. For the secondary information concept Goal, the concept Objective is listed, and for Objective, the concept Initiative is listed. The column for Initiative is filled with the primary information concept Strategy. A relationship between two information concepts is bi-directional. For this reason, not every information concept needs to be included in the other's column (see Table 8-10 and Figure 8-8 for an example).

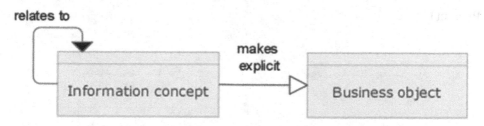

Figure 8-7. *Relationship between information concepts and business objects*

To graphically represent an information concept in a model, the business object concept is used. There is currently no separate concept in the modeling language that is a direct translation of the information concept. The definition of a business object shows that this concept can contain information that is essential to an organization, making it a plausible concept to use.

Only occasionally, business objects represent actual instances of information produced and consumed by behavior elements such as business processes [12].

Figure 8-8 shows the relationship between the primary information concept Strategy and the secondary concepts Goal, Objective, and Initiative. Among them, Goal, Objective, and Initiative are interrelated. The information concept Strategy has a *compositional relationship* with Goal and Objective because the secondary information concepts exist only because of the fact that Strategy exists. The *aggregation relationship*

111

between Strategy and Initiative arises because Initiative can exist without the primary information concept Strategy. This is due to the fact that the secondary information concept Initiative does not depend on Strategy alone. It can also have a relationship with, for example, the information concept Portfolio (or in some cases also with the information concept Project).

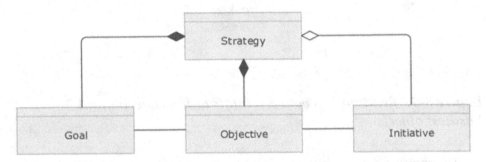

Figure 8-8. *Visual representation of information concepts and their interrelationships*

In addition to creating a diagram with the information concepts and their interrelationships, it is also possible to display all the information concepts in alphabetical order and spread across multiple rows. The interrelationships are then lost in the model, but an overall view of all the information concepts can be just as valuable at some times as the separate diagrams of the individual information concepts. The form in which the Information Map is visualized depends entirely on what works for the architect and the organization. An example of part of an Information Map is included in Appendix A: Example Information Map.

Information Concept/Business Process Matrix

A completed Information Concept/Business Process Matrix makes it possible to determine which information concepts are used by which business processes. This matrix can be used to map information flows. An Information Concept/Business Process Matrix shows where information circulates in the organization. The power of this matrix can be further enhanced by creating an Application/Information Concept Matrix or an Application/Business Process Matrix (see Section 8.2.1.4). The combination of two matrices (the Information Concept/Business Process Matrix combined with one of the other two matrices mentioned above) results in a detailed representation of the information concepts used in the organization. For each information concept, it can be shown which application uses which information concept and which process accesses the information concepts. This is useful during application replacement projects or when processes are adapted. The impact on the information flow can be determined in both situations.

Table 8-11. *Information Concept/Business Process Matrix*

	Business processes					
	Process A	Process B	Process C	Process D	Process E	Process F
Information concepts						
Agreement			X		X	
License	X		X	X		
Order		X		X		X
Payment	X	X			X	X

As with all matrices, a more graphical representation of the Information Concept/Business Process Matrix can be created: an Information Concept/Business Process Diagram. Because the information concepts are related to other elements (in this case, business processes), the architecture tool can create a cross section and present it using colors (creating a *color view*).

Figure 8-9 shows which business processes belong to which business functions and where each information concept is used in which business processes. To illustrate, the Agreement information concept is used by business processes C and E.

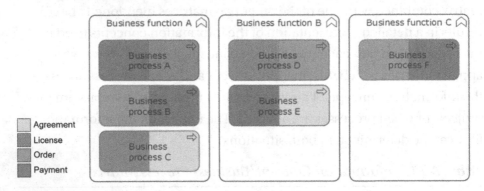

Figure 8-9. *Information Concept/Business Process Diagram color view*

The ability to create color views is a powerful feature of the architecture tool. They often show at a glance the relationships that exist between elements in the diagram and elements that are related to them but not visible in the diagram. In effect, a color view adds an extra layer or dimension to an existing diagram. The ability to use color views is one of the potential requirements when purchasing an architecture tool (see Chapter 6, Section 6.4).

8.2.1.4. Applications

Table 8-12. *Deliverables of the focus area Applications*

Deliverable	Description
Application Portfolio Catalog	Listing of applications in use, both internal and external (e.g., cloud services purchased)
Application/Information Concept Matrix	Cross-mapping of applications and information concepts
Application/Business Process Matrix	Cross-mapping of applications and business processes

An application component is a modular and self-contained piece of software or software system that provides specific application functionality. Application components are used to model individual applications or software modules within a larger application or system. By using application components effectively, Enterprise Architects can optimize the application portfolio, design integration solutions, promote modularity, and ensure that applications are aligned with the organization's strategic objectives and user requirements.

Application components are used to represent individual applications within the enterprise application portfolio. An Enterprise Architect can use these components to assess the relevance, redundancy, and value of each application, helping to optimize the application portfolio and make informed decisions about application retirement or consolidation. This is called application portfolio management.

Application components help architects evaluate the technology stack used in different applications. This facilitates technology rationalization efforts, allowing architects to standardize technology platforms and minimize technology redundancies. They also help manage the application lifecycle. Architects can track the development, deployment, maintenance, and retirement of each component to ensure that applications remain current and aligned with business needs, enabling application lifecycle management.

Application Portfolio Catalog

Creating an Application Portfolio Catalog helps provide a complete view of all the applications that exist and are being used in an organization. An Application Portfolio Catalog also helps provide insight into where in the organization applications with similar functionality are being used. For example, think about situations where application components are used to run reports, to take screenshots, or to store and process customer data. It is more common than one might think to have application components in use within an organization that provide virtually the same functionality.

The lack of a complete view of all application components can cause problems. For example, different departments may request a variety of applications, while the desired functionality is often already available within the organization. Since the availability or unavailability of the requested functionality cannot be directly verified, the request for a new application component is approved (often too quickly). This eventually leads to overpopulation of the application landscape and the need for an organization to rationalize applications (often after years).

A second problem that can arise in the absence of an Application Portfolio Catalog is that costs are incurred that are not fully visible. For example, an organization may find that a lot of money is being spent on software licenses, but it is not entirely clear what those license costs consist of. The lack of an Application Portfolio Catalog plays a major role in the inability to get a clear picture of license costs. Often, it is only after an Application Portfolio Catalog is created that it becomes clear that the license costs consist of duplicate application functionality. By removing application components with duplicate (or sometimes triple or quadruple!) functionality from the application landscape, license costs can be significantly reduced.

To arrive at an Application Portfolio Catalog, the following questions can be asked. The best place to start is the IT department (and/or vendor support desk).

Questions to ask the IT department include:

- Is a Configuration Management Database (CMDB) in use?

- What off-the-shelf applications are used?

- Are there any special or noteworthy application components in use?

- Are contracts for purchased licenses available for review?

Of course, it is also useful to interview people from different departments. Examples of questions to ask include:

- What software is used to perform the work?

- Is specific functionality needed to perform the job?

- What are the steps involved in performing the work?

When you ask people in your organization what software they use, they often mention one or two applications.

The trick is to ask follow-up questions.

Ask how they use the software, how they use it for day-to-day operations, etc.

I have seen people respond to this question what software they use by saying that they use a customer relationship management product. However, when I actually sat down with the employees in question and watched them work, it turned out that in addition to the customer relationship management application, they were also using an office suite (word processing for writing letters, sending e-mail messages, and creating overviews of customer activity in a spreadsheet application), a PDF reader for reading received documents, and a web browser for accessing the Internet to look up information.

Therefore, asking follow-up questions provides a lot of additional insight.

Once the information has been gathered and captured in the Architecture Repository, it is time to create an Application Portfolio Catalog. There are several ways to visualize the big picture.

Table 8-13. *Application Portfolio Catalog*

Application component name	Application location	Application function	Supplier	CIA score
Application component A	On-premise	Function A	Supplier A	2-2-3
Application component A	On-premise	Function B	Supplier A	2-2-3
Application component B	On-premise	Function A	Supplier B	3-1-1
Application component C	On-premise	Function C	Supplier C	3-3-3
Application component D	Cloud	Function C	Supplier D	1-1-1
Application component E	Cloud	Function D	Supplier D	1-2-1

A spreadsheet can be used to keep track of the application components used in the organization, with the name of the application component listed on each row. It also records whether the application component is a locally installed product or a Software-as-a-Service (SaaS) product purchased from the cloud. Knowing who the application vendor is or what the confidentiality, integrity, and availability (CIA) score[1] is also provides valuable information. The CIA score can be used to determine whether an application component is mission-critical or not. Ensure that all information is also captured in the repository.

Instead of capturing the information in a spreadsheet, it can also be visualized in a diagram.

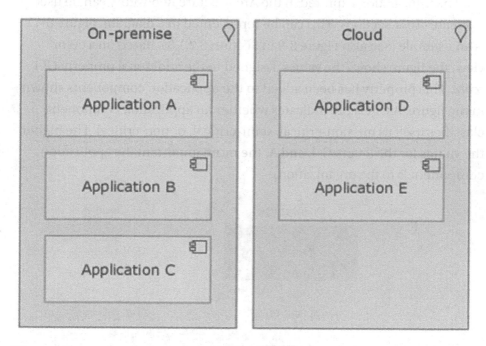

Figure 8-10. Application Portfolio Diagram

---

[1] The CIA score comes from information security. It refers to the information rather than the application itself. Since information is often accessed through an application, in practice the CIA score is usually assigned to the application rather than the information being accessed.

The diagram in Figure 8-10 visualizes the same information as Table 8-13. A graphical representation sometimes captures the imagination more than the somewhat static tabular representation. In discussions with stakeholders within the organization, it is sometimes better to use a list view. There are also times when a graphical representation is more appropriate, such as when making presentations. In this case, the graphical view is preferred over the list view.

The information captured in the Architecture Repository can be used to create cross-sections. This can be represented in a diagram. Figure 8-11 is an example (see also Figure 8-9 in Section 8.2.1.3). Based on a color view, the figure shows the values assigned to the additional property *CIA score*. This property has been added to the application components shown in the figure. A CIA score indicates whether an application component classifies itself as mission-critical, semi-critical, or non-critical. The higher the values for the letters C, I, and A, the more important the application component is to the organization.

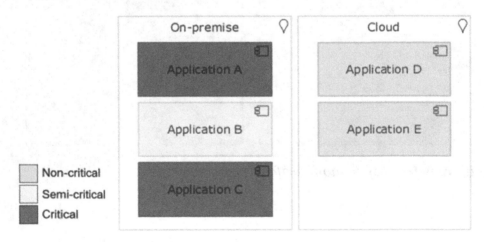

Figure 8-11. *Application Portfolio Diagram colored by CIA score*

Figure 8-11 shows that two application components (Application component A and C) in the on-premises location received a high CIA score and were therefore considered mission-critical. Application component B was found to be semi-critical, and the two application components (Application component D and E) purchased as a cloud service were considered non-critical.

The more additional information that can be added to the Application Portfolio Catalog, the more meaningful the catalog becomes. This greatly increases the reusability of an Application Portfolio Catalog (or diagram).

Application/Information Concept Matrix

An Application/Information Concept Matrix shows which application components allow access to which information concepts. The cross-mapping between application component and information concepts visualizes where an information concept is made available for consultation.

Section 8.2.1.3 indicated that creating an Application/Information Concept Matrix is a valuable complement to the Information Concept/Business Process Matrix. When the two matrices are combined, an overall picture of the use of information concepts emerges. Merging the two matrices provides insight into which application components are used to access specific information and which processes are used to do so. It also provides insight into where in the organization (within which departments or business units) these processes are being performed. By using these two matrices, it is possible to trace where and how information is used and accessed down to the departmental level.

Table 8-14. *Application/Information Concept Matrix*

	Information concepts				
	Agreement	**License**	**Order**	**Payment**	**Medical history**
Applications					
Application A	X	X			
Application B			X		
Application C				X	
Application D		X	X		
Application E					X

An Application/Information Concept Matrix can also be used for additional purposes. One such additional purpose is to provide insight into which application components require additional security measures. This is typically done using the CIA score. Certain types of information (such as sensitive personal information) cannot be made available to everyone and often require additional security measures. In most organizations, application components that provide access to sensitive information are subject to additional integrity and confidentiality requirements. Nine times out of ten, this results in a high CIA score.

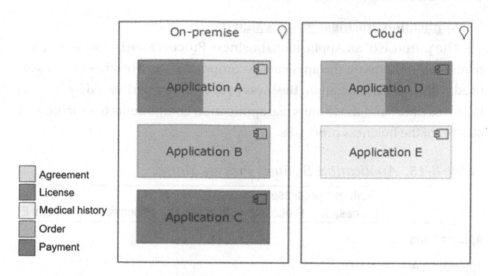

Figure 8-12. *Application/Information Concept Diagram color view*

An Application/Information Concept Matrix can help determine which application components should meet the additional requirements from a security perspective. The addition of the CIA score to the Application Portfolio Catalog is a useful tool in this regard.

Figure 8-12 shows the relationship between the application components and the information concepts that can be accessed. To illustrate, Application component E enables the retrieval of historical medical data. This type of information falls into the category of sensitive personal information and has additional security requirements. The CIA score for this application component generates high values for confidentiality and integrity.

Of course, many more cross sections can be created based on the information captured in the Application Portfolio Catalog. The example shown in Figure 8-12 is just one of many uses of the Application Portfolio Catalog.

Application/Business Process Matrix

The purpose of an Application/Business Process Matrix is to show the relationships between the application components and business processes used within the organization. Business processes are performed by business units, and these units use application components to execute and automate the business processes.

Table 8-15. *Application/Business Process Matrix*

| | Business processes | | | | |
	Process A	Process B	Process C	Process D	Process E
Applications					
Application A	X				
Application B	X	X			
Application C				X	
Application D					X
Application E		X		X	

Take, for example, a cross-mapping between application components and business processes. This provides insight into the application support required to execute the processes. If an application component is associated with multiple business processes, it is wise to ensure that sufficient support is available for the application component in question. If such an application component is (temporarily) unavailable, it will most likely have a significant (negative) impact on the continuity of the organization.

An Application/Business Process Matrix also reveals whether application components are missing or perhaps duplicate. Empty cells in the matrix indicate missing application components for existing business processes (see Business Process C in Table 8-15). This may mean that these processes are being performed manually. In these situations, there are benefits to be gained by automating the business processes through the use of application components.

If it is determined that application components are being deployed multiple times (see Application components A and B, B and E, C and E in Table 8-15), this may lead to an application rationalization initiative. Cleaning up (removing) duplicate application components can result in significant financial savings.[2]

8.2.1.5. Technology

Table 8-16. *Deliverables of the focus area Technology*

Deliverable	Description
Technology Portfolio Catalog	Enumeration of (server) systems in use, both internal and external (e.g., technological cloud services)
Technology/Application Matrix	Cross-mapping of used (server) systems and applications
Technology/Application Function Map	Mapping technology services to application functionality

Technology Portfolio Catalog

A Technology Portfolio Catalog is designed to identify and track all technology components in use within the organization. Examples include hardware (devices) and infrastructure software (system software). An agreed-upon technology portfolio supports the lifecycle management of

---

[2] The focus of this book is not on implementing application rationalization, so this initiative is not discussed here.

technology products and releases. The technology components collected in a Technology Portfolio Catalog can also be used to define technology standards.

The TOGAF Standard provides two definitions of what is meant by a technology component.

---

1. A technology building block. A generic infrastructure technology that supports and enables application or data components (directly or indirectly) by providing technology services.

2. An encapsulation of technology infrastructure that represents a class of technology product or specific technology product [1].

Creating a Technology Portfolio Catalog starts with making an appointment with the Configuration Management Database (CMDB) administrator. This person will most likely have a (reasonably) up-to-date record of all the server systems (devices) used in the organization. Ask for the list of technology components and document them in the Architecture Repository. Complete the components with information such as operating system software, version numbers, vendors, and the purpose of the technology component.

If a CMDB administrator is not available, it is possible to go into the server room in person, accompanied, of course, by someone with appropriate access privileges. The inventory of devices is then done by hand. Does the organization use outsourced services? If so, it is a good idea to find out who the contacts are at the vendors, based on existing support contracts. Find out what agreements have been made with the suppliers and obtain information about the technology components for which they provide services to the organization.

If a CMDB exists within the organization, it is and will remain the source for the primary collection of technology components. An export of the information contained in the CMDB can be performed a few times a year. The Architecture Repository can then be updated based on the exported data.

Some key questions that can be asked to arrive at a Technology Portfolio Map are:

- Is there a list of technology components in use?

- Is a Configuration Management Database (CMDB) in use?

- What is the purpose and role of the technology component?

- What off-the-shelf technology components are used?

- Is it a physical device or is it virtual?

- Are there any special or notable technology components in use?

- Are there any contracts available for review regarding the purchased technology component?

- Is the component within the walls of the organization (is it owned by the organization)?

- Is the technology component purchased as a service from a vendor?

Additional and more detailed questions (what operating system is running on the device, what version is being used, etc.) can be asked after the main questions have been answered.

It is quite possible that the inventory will produce an overview similar to Table 8-17. The values used in the columns are for illustrative purposes.

Table 8-17. *Technology Portfolio Catalog*

Technology component	Operating system	OS Version number	Supplier	Purpose
Device A	Microsoft Windows Server	2019	Supplier A	Database server
Device B	Microsoft Windows Server	2022	Supplier A	Database server
Device C	Microsoft Windows Server	2022	Supplier A	File server
Device D	Microsoft Windows Server	2012 (R2)	Supplier B	Web server

The Technology Portfolio Catalog can also be visualized using a diagram (Figure 8-13).

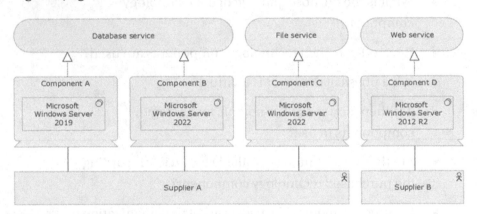

Figure 8-13. *Technology Portfolio Diagram*

The choice between a catalog and a diagram is usually a matter of personal preference. A catalog is preferred when the amount of additional information exceeds two columns (from the Technology Portfolio Catalog) of additional information. The more features that are visualized in a diagram, the more cluttered the diagram becomes.

Technology/Application Matrix

Once the Technology Portfolio Catalog has been created, attention can be turned to creating a Technology/Application Matrix. As described in Section 8.2.1.2, a cross-mapping is a relationship between two variables that shows the cause-and-effect relationship between them. With the right architecture tool, cross-mapping between two maps is easy.

To create a Technology/Application Matrix, the technology components must be mapped to the previously inventoried application components.

Table 8-18. *Technology/Application Matrix*

	Application component				
	Application component A	Application component B	Application component C	Application component D	Application component E
Technology component					
Device A	X				
Device B		X			
Device C			X		
Device D				X	
Device E	X				X

In the example from Table 8-18, we can see that Device E has a relationship with two application components, A and E. Using the insight gained after creating a Technology/Application Matrix, it is possible to further investigate whether it is desirable for both Application components A and E to be available through the deployment of Device E. After doing the research, a first observation could be that Device E is the replacement for Device A (and therefore Application component A is installed). A second observation might be that Application component E is highly dependent on Application component A. It is even possible to make a third observation, namely, that the first two observations are both applicable and accurate.

Many scenarios are possible, and it is useful to use the insights provided by a Technology/Application Matrix to investigate the reasons for striking or anomalous findings.

Technology/Application Function Map

In fact, a technology component does not directly provide a service to an application. It does so through a *technology service*. In creating the Technology Portfolio Catalog, it was noted that filling in the *purpose* column was valuable. In addition to providing insight into the purpose of a technology component, the input from this column can also be used in the context of cross-mapping with application functionality. Incorporating the purpose column from the Technology Portfolio Catalog into a Technology/Application Function Map and articulating it in a different, more action-oriented way creates a technology services column. Based on services, a technology component can be related to one or more application components.

By the way, the Technology/Application Function Map is not a standard architecture deliverable according to the TOGAF Standard. However, the framework provides the room to tailor it to the needs of the organization. The use of a Technology/Application Function Map provides valuable insight, and it is recommended that it be created and used.

Take the *Application function* column from the Application Portfolio Catalog, and place it next to the Technology service column in the Technology/Application Function Map. This allows you to see if the intended purpose of the technology component matches the function of the application component.

Table 8-19. *Technology/Application Function Map*

Technology component	Technology service[3]	Application name	Application function
Device A	Database service	Application component A	Function A
Device B	Database service	Application component B	Function A
Device C	File storage service	Application component C	Function C
Device D	Web service	Application component D (cloud)	Function C

The example Technology/Application Function Map (Table 8-19) shows that Devices A and B both provide a database service to Application components A and B, and the same application functionality is used by Application components A and B. It is plausible to assume that this is database functionality, such as gathering information, running reports, or analyzing data.

What is noticeable is the use of an application functionality called Function C. This functionality is provided by Application components C and D and is supported by Devices C and D. However, Device C provides a file storage functionality as opposed to the web service functionality provided by Device D.

The conclusion that can be drawn from this fact is that Device D (the web service) most likely also provides a data storage capability. While Device C does this through a file system, Device D may provide the same service through a web interface.

---

[3] This is the original *Purpose* column from the Technology Portfolio Catalog (see Table 8-17).

The question is whether it is desirable to maintain two environments that provide the same service. The answer to this question, by the way, is not necessarily that it would not be wise. The fact that it comes to light when a Technology/Application Function Map is completed provides an opportunity to start the conversation with the organization about this observation.

After completing the *Information* step of the first stage of the Enterprise Architecture Implementation Wheel, there should now be an architecture repository containing a large number of catalogs, matrices, diagrams, and maps. There will also be many objects registered, such as business units, business processes, information concepts, applications, and technology components. The architecture deliverables and concepts represent the organization across all architecture domains. They provide a basic picture of what the organization looks like, what it does, and how it does it. This valuable information can be used to communicate with the organization and its stakeholders.

8.2.2. Stakeholders

The stakeholder concept is fundamental to representing an individual, group, or organization that has an interest in the outcome of an architecture effort. Stakeholders are critical to the success of any Enterprise Architecture initiative because they provide input, have concerns, and influence decision-making throughout the architecture development process. Enterprise Architects use the stakeholder concept to identify and analyze the concerns and interests of various stakeholders. Understanding stakeholder needs and expectations helps define architecture requirements and ensures that the architecture effectively addresses business goals.

Stakeholders are actively involved throughout the architecture development process. Enterprise Architects work with stakeholders to gather information, obtain feedback, and validate architectural decisions. Effective stakeholder engagement results in a shared understanding of business goals and ensures buy-in for the proposed architecture.

The stakeholder concept facilitates effective communication with various groups within the organization. Architects use the concept to document stakeholder relationships, communication channels, and key roles within the architecture effort. It helps manage expectations and ensure that stakeholders are kept informed of progress and results.

Stakeholders play a critical role in assessing the impact of architecture decisions on various business areas. By understanding stakeholder perspectives, architects can identify potential risks and opportunities associated with architectural changes and align the architecture with the organization's strategy. The primary goal of Enterprise Architecture is to align IT with business goals. Understanding stakeholder perspectives helps architects prioritize initiatives and allocate resources to projects that deliver the most value to the organization and its stakeholders.

Stakeholders are an important source of requirements for the architecture. By interacting with stakeholders, architects can elicit and document their needs, which become the basis for developing architectural models and solutions. The stakeholder concept helps architects make informed decisions. By considering the interests and concerns of different stakeholders, architects can balance conflicting requirements and ensure that architectural decisions are well accepted and aligned with business priorities.

The stakeholder concept is closely related to governance in Enterprise Architecture. By understanding who the stakeholders are and what their interests are, architects can establish governance mechanisms to address their concerns, maintain transparency, and ensure accountability.

Being able to communicate properly with stakeholders – the key players within the organization – is essential. To identify these key players in an organization, *stakeholder management* can be applied. Stakeholder management is the process of identifying and understanding the needs, interests, and expectations of an organization's various stakeholders, and planning and implementing actions to address those interests and improve cooperation and communication with them.

In the context of the TOGAF Standard, stakeholder management is an essential part of Enterprise Architecture development and is explicitly reflected in what the framework calls the *Architecture Development Cycle*[4]. Stakeholder management is one of the most important factors in the success of an Enterprise Architecture initiative.

Table 8-20. *Deliverables of stage one – Document/Stakeholders*

Deliverable	Description
Stakeholder Analysis Model	Visualizes the needs and expectations of key stakeholders
Stakeholder Map	Listing of key stakeholders, classification, and key concerns
Communications Plan	Identifies the (groups of) stakeholders to be included in the communication regarding the implementation of the Enterprise Architecture

The main steps that can be taken in relation to stakeholder management are described in Sections 8.2.2.1 to 8.2.2.5.

---

[4] This refers to an iteration through the Architecture Development Method (ADM). Refer to Chapter 2, Section 2.3.1.1, for more information.

8.2.2.1. Identify Key Stakeholders

The first and most important part of stakeholder management is *identifying stakeholders* and their roles and responsibilities. This can be done through interviews, workshops, surveys, and other feedback-gathering techniques. Consider who will be affected by the implementation of an Enterprise Architecture, who will have influence or power over it, or who will have a stake in whether or not the implementation is successful.

These may include (senior) management, various roles in the project organization, roles in the customer organization, alliance partners, system developers, suppliers, customers, etc. When identifying stakeholders, it is important not to look only at one's own organization, as there may be influential stakeholders outside the organization. This has already been taken into account during the creation of the Organization Map (see Section 8.2.1.1). In addition, it is advisable not to limit the view to the mainstream and more formal groups; informal stakeholder groups can be just as influential as the formal ones. The Business Roles Map (see Section 8.2.1.1) plays a supporting role here by providing an overview of the roles that exist in the organization.

Ask questions to arrive at the most complete list of stakeholders possible:

- Who makes the decisions?

- Who are the go-to people in the department or unit?

- Who else has influence?

- Who has specific or specialized skills that are needed?

The answers to these questions provide insight into the decision-making hierarchy, as well as who has and can exercise influence within the organization. In some cases, this is a person who is often called upon to express an opinion or determine a direction or course of action. These are the influencers. They often attend important meetings and are valued by their peers and superiors. Influencers do not necessarily have to be in a formal position of power like managers.

8.2.2.2. Analyze Needs and Expectations

After identifying stakeholders, the architect must *analyze* these groups to understand their needs and expectations. This can help prioritize their requirements and determine the best way to design the architecture to meet their needs. This can be done using a Stakeholder Analysis Model [21]. An example is shown in Table 8-21.

Table 8-21. Stakeholder Analysis Model

Stakeholder group	Stakeholder	Ability to disrupt change	Current understanding	Required understanding	Current commitment	Required commitment	Required support
CIO	Jane Doe	H	M	H	L	M	H
CFO	John Smith	M	M	M	L	M	M

When creating a Stakeholder Analysis Model, it is important to find out how much influence the stakeholder has over a number of issues. To gain insight into this, a Stakeholder Power Grid (Figure 8-14) can be created.

8.2.2.3. Classify Stakeholders

Stakeholder *classification* is best done based on the level of power and influence they have and the level of interest and/or involvement. A simple matrix table can be used to assign a classification to a particular stakeholder.

The Stakeholder Power Grid (Figure 8-14) shows which classifications can be assigned to stakeholders. Each classification comes with a set of requirements regarding the stakeholder's communication needs. What information does the stakeholder need? What is the appropriate frequency of communication? What is the most appropriate method of communication? The answers to these questions form the basis of the Communications Plan (see Table 8-23).

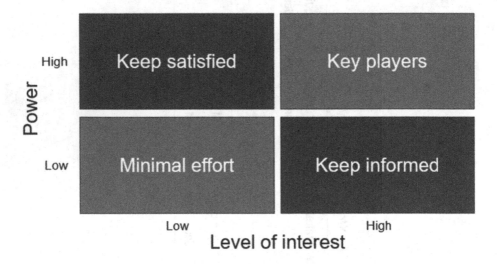

Figure 8-14. *Stakeholder Power Grid*

A Stakeholder Power Grid is divided into four quadrants. Each quadrant has specific attributes that apply to the stakeholders in that quadrant.

Key players: This classification indicates that these are stakeholders with a high level of interest and power within the organization. Therefore, the frequency of communication to this group of stakeholders will be the highest. An example of this stakeholder classification is data and process owners.

Keep satisfied: Stakeholders classified as Keep satisfied have the same level of power in the organization as the Key players, but their level of interest is lower. Therefore, this group can be informed with a slightly lower frequency. An organization's C-level functions fall into this classification.

Keep informed: The level of interest among this group of stakeholders is high, but the power they can exercise within the organization is lower. Nevertheless, it is wise to keep this group informed on a regular basis. For this group, the choice is between informing them by email or in the form of a meeting (physical or digital). An example of a stakeholder in this classification is the program manager.

Minimal effort: Although this term has a negative connotation, this is far from the intention. It refers to the fact that stakeholders in this group have a low level of interest and power. However, this group can still contain stakeholders that are very important to the implementation of the Enterprise Architecture. The Employees group falls into this classification.

The assigned classifications are used in the creation of the Communications Plan (see Section 8.2.2.5).

8.2.2.4. Stakeholder Map

Another useful tool for stakeholder management is the creation of a Stakeholder Map. A Stakeholder Map contains not only the stakeholders and their classification, but also the *key concerns* of the stakeholders.

A final part of the stakeholder map is a reference to the different catalogs, matrices, diagrams, and maps that may be needed for a specific (group of) stakeholder(s).

Table 8-22. *Stakeholder Map*

Stakeholder	Key concerns	Class	Catalogs, matrices, and diagrams
CxO (CEO, CFO, CIO, COO)	The high-level drivers, goals, and objectives of the organization, and how these are translated into an effective process to advance the business	Keep satisfied	Strategy/Goal Matrix Goal/Objective Matrix

Stakeholder management is a critical part of developing Enterprise Architecture and therefore one of the key success factors. Completing the Stakeholder Map provides an important source document that can be used frequently. The stakeholders listed in the Stakeholder Map need to be approached and informed appropriately. A Communications Plan is used for this purpose.

8.2.2.5. Communications Plan

It is important to communicate effectively with stakeholders. One way to do this is to create a Communications Plan. Such a plan ensures effective communication of the necessary information to the relevant stakeholders at the right time. It is therefore one of the critical success factors (CSF) for a sound implementation of an Enterprise Architecture [22].

The Communications Plan should describe the communication needs of each stakeholder group, such as the information they need, the frequency of communication, and the methods for sharing information. It should also state the purpose of the communication to the stakeholders. Of course, this will not be the same for each stakeholder group, and this distinction needs to be well defined.

The Stakeholder Power Grid (Figure 8-14) shows which classifications can be given to stakeholders. With each classification comes a set of requirements regarding the communication needs of the stakeholders. It is important to include the moments – especially the frequency of these moments – at which stakeholders are informed or updated.

The TOGAF Standard indicates that the scope of a Communications Plan is limited to key stakeholders. In my view, communication does not stop there.

It is precisely by communicating to the entire organization what the expected impact of implementing the Enterprise Architecture will be that everyone becomes involved. It becomes more of everyone, rather than just those directly involved. This strengthens the acceptance of the Enterprise Architecture as well as working with architecture.

There are two components that are essential to include in a Communications Plan.

The first is to include and interpret what everyone's role will be in implementing the Enterprise Architecture. This does not need to be detailed; an overall articulation in terms of roles to be fulfilled is sufficient. If people can see themselves in the roles outlined, with the associated roles and responsibilities, it will be easier to buy into the implementation. Everyone likes to make a meaningful contribution. What is sometimes missing in practice is the interpretation of that meaning. Once the meaning is unclear, people's enthusiasm for making the desired contribution diminishes. So be clear and precise in your descriptions.

The second essential part of the Communications Plan is to schedule consultation moments when the organization as a whole is updated or informed about the progress of the implementation and the method(s) to be used or to be used. Transparency in the approach is very important.

Of course, this does not always mean that all employees are informed at the same time; it is certainly possible to create a division into small(er) groups.

Once the Communications Plan for Enterprise Architecture implementation has been created, the architect must implement it to foster effective communication and collaboration. From then on, stakeholders are regularly updated on the progress of the implementation, and feedback sessions are offered as opportunities for stakeholders to provide input.

Table 8-23. *Communications Plan*

Stakeholder group	Class	Communication goals	Communication method	Communication frequency
CxO	Keep satisfied	Provide insight into how the high-level drivers, goals, and objectives are translated into the Enterprise Architecture	Meeting	Every fortnight

(continued)

Table 8-23. (*continued*)

Stakeholder group	Class	Communication goals	Communication method	Communication frequency
Data and process owners	Key players	Ensure the consistent use and governance of the organization's business, data, application, and technology assets	Meeting	Monthly
Program manager	Keep informed	On-time, on-budget delivery of the change initiatives that will lead to the implementation of the Enterprise Architecture	Meeting	Monthly
Employees	Minimal effort	Assess the impact of the implementation of the Enterprise Architecture with regard to the day-to-day duties and tasks	Email message, alternated with meeting	Monthly
Human resources	Minimal effort	Ensure that the roles and actors who are required to support the implementation of the Enterprise Architecture are available	Email message	Quarterly

A standard Communications Plan (Table 8-23) often looks rather static and business-like, and usually does not provide the most effective means of communication in practice. It is therefore advisable to explore options for additional means of communication.

A more effective way of communicating might be to use appealing and sophisticated visuals and designs that can be used to capture and hold the attention of stakeholders. Common forms of this are presentations and infographics, but posters or specially decorated rooms where the information is highlighted can also help. It is a good idea to enlist the help of colleagues in the communications or graphic design department to help get the message across. They know best how to speak the language of the organization.

After completing the *Documentation* stage of the Enterprise Architecture Implementation Wheel, it is very important to make sure that the inventoried information is being used. Make sure that the various catalogs, matrices, diagrams, and maps are being used in all sorts of ways. Because the architecture products provide insight, it becomes easier for the organization to make decisions. After all, an informed decision is easier to make than a gut decision. Finally, the use of architecture products will not go unnoticed by the board or management. Now is the time to get a seat at the board table.

8.3. Define

The second stage of the Implementation Wheel is *Define*. This stage consists of three steps: *Maturity*, *Framework*, and *Strategy*. The first step, Maturity, addresses the use of a maturity model and its associated maturity levels. This step also provides a guide for determining the current and desired maturity of the architecture. Step two (Framework) elaborates on the realization of a basic framework (basic principles, quality requirements, and standards), and step three (Strategy) explains how to define concrete drivers, goals, objectives, and initiatives.

Table 8-24. *Second stage of the Enterprise Architecture Implementation Wheel*

Document		Define			Execute		Control
Information	Stakeholders	Maturity	Framework	Strategy	Strategy	Roadmap	Measure progress

8.3.1. Maturity

Table 8-25. *Deliverables of stage two – Define/Maturity*

Deliverable	Description
Maturity model	Visualizes an organization's architecture maturity across five maturity elements, plotted against five maturity levels

Introducing working under architecture, or perhaps more accurately, working with architecture, is a complex and time-consuming matter. An organization is accustomed to doing things a certain way. It is then difficult (but certainly not impossible) to change what is ingrained in the system and culture of the organization.

Introducing working with architecture therefore requires a lot of time and effort. It requires a long breath, but when the first changes become visible, it gives new energy to continue on the chosen path.

Some time ago, I worked for an organization where architectural thinking was virtually nonexistent. The organization operated as it had for years. Oddly enough, it had never really caused any major problems or deficiencies in the past.

Prompted by a change in the composition of the organization's board of directors, there was a desire to bring more structure to the way we worked. This was necessary because the lack of structure was making certain actions and processes less efficient. This resulted in longer lead times and ultimately less satisfied customers with the services provided.

Working with architecture, or the desire to do so, was born.

One of the first things an architect should determine is the maturity level of the organization he or she is working for. This will help shape the approach to putting architecture on the map and evolving it.

Not every organization is able (or rather, wants) to describe its current level of architectural thinking. The same can be said for an organization that expresses its maturity in dealing with architecture. This probably has something to do with not wanting to be seen as an organization that hasn't gone far enough in putting architecture on the map. More often than not, an organization doesn't want to be seen as the one that can't get to a minimum level of structured work. Organizations are often vague when asked about their level of structured working. However, it is important to determine the maturity level of architectural thinking and working with architecture in order to allow the organization to grow. What is useful in these cases is the introduction of a maturity model. Such a model allows the organization to start the conversation about its maturity using clearly defined maturity levels. These levels guide the organization from one level to the next.

8.3.1.1. Maturity Model

An Enterprise Architecture Maturity Model is a framework used to assess the maturity and effectiveness of an organization's use of Enterprise Architecture. The model describes the various stages of maturity and provides a structured way to evaluate where an organization stands in terms of Enterprise Architecture.

The purpose of an Enterprise Architecture Maturity Model is to help organizations improve the implementation and execution of Enterprise Architecture and become more mature. It is also used to understand which areas need improvement. By understanding the organization's maturity level, the organization can make targeted improvements to the implementation of Enterprise Architecture to achieve better business results.

There are several Enterprise Architecture Maturity Models available. Each model has its own set of evaluation criteria. It is important to select a model that is a good fit for the organization. For example, if the architect works for a fairly informal organization, do not choose a formal maturity model. Such a formal model is more likely to be intimidating than to be used and adopted. As much as possible, match the model to be used to the way the organization works, the people who work there, and the culture that prevails.

Enterprise Architecture Maturity Models are often based on the Capability Maturity Model Integration (CMMI) framework [23]. CMMI is originally a standardized model for assessing and improving the processes used in software development and other engineering disciplines. Today, the model is also regularly used to indicate the maturity of an Enterprise Architecture.

Of course, there are several ways to build a maturity model. An example of a good model to use and apply is shown in Table 8-26 [24]. A more detailed elaboration of this model can be found in Appendix B: Example Maturity Model.

Table 8-26. Maturity model

	Ad hoc	Repeatable	Defined	Managed	Optimal
Strategy and vision	Architecture activities are not formally initiated and happen ad hoc	The organization has started drafting a vision for EA	EA deployment is clearly defined, including governance roles and responsibilities	The EA is evaluated, and adjustments are identified to improve the EA	Action plans are proactively implemented to increase EA effectiveness based on measured data
Architecture governance	The need to define processes and standards is recognized	The need for governance has been identified	Architecture governance is defined (a consultative body has been created)	The communication process is revised to improve EA activity	The organization collaborates with similar organizations exchanging ideas to improve their EA

	Ad hoc	Repeatable	Defined	Managed	Optimal
Architecture method and process	Architecture processes are ad hoc and inconsistent	The architecture method is beginning to be reused to capture crucial EA information	Templates are used so that capture of information is consistent	EA is used to guide organizational development	Business influences technology and technology influences business
Architecture deliverables	The documentation of business drivers, goals and objectives, architecture standards, etc. are not formally defined	Drivers, goals, and objectives have been identified	Classification of existing standards is consistent	Documentation of drivers, goals, and objectives has become a standard activity	Captured business and technology information is used to proactively identify technology that will improve business operations
Business alignment	The organization recognizes that staff need to become more familiar with working with architecture	The organization has started raising awareness and understanding of EA concepts and processes	The organization starts to operate as a team, using the defined architecture and standards	Staff throughout the organization have a good understanding of the architecture principles	Departments work together as contributors to the architecture and its processes

8.3.1.2. Maturity Levels

A maturity model based on CMMI defines five levels of Enterprise Architecture maturity. These are shown in the columns of Table 8-26.

Ad hoc: Frameworks and standards have not yet been established, and the architecture process is generally conducted in an informal manner. The organization is aware of the benefits that Enterprise Architecture can provide, but has not yet defined a process to track and monitor the evolution of the architecture process. The organization relies on the knowledge and skills of individual employees. A strategy exists, but has not yet been translated into implementation.

Repeatable: The architecture process is formalized, and there is a vision for the architecture. The architecture process is repeatable, and templates and standards are being developed. The need for adherence to architectural frameworks is recognized by senior management, and efforts are made to formalize it through process capture. Metrics are also being captured to evaluate the process. The organization's strategy is beginning to be translated into concrete goals and objectives. The words *enterprise* and *architecture* are used with some regularity in conversations at the strategic level.

Defined: The architecture framework to be used has been determined, and there is a formally defined process for adhering to the architecture process. The architecture framework is now formalized, and standards are widely used within the organization. There is a roadmap for the evolution of the architecture, and related activities are performed in accordance with the roadmap. Metrics are maintained and monitored for the purpose of evolving the architecture process.

Managed: Measurement data is actively used to improve and refine the architecture process. Data is analyzed and used to drive architecture performance. The Enterprise Architecture is invariably used to inform the organization's strategy. Adherence to the architecture framework is a standard activity within the organization.

Optimal: The architecture process is mature; the organization has drivers, goals, and objectives created based on the application of Enterprise Architecture. Continuous improvements are made to the architecture process, and projects and other initiatives can no longer proceed without Enterprise Architecture input. Work is also done outside the boundaries of one's own organization to improve and refine the architecture together with similar organizations. Experiences are shared and suggestions for improving processes are discussed.

A maturity model is a powerful tool. Its use enables an organization to identify opportunities for growth and development. By translating the activities associated with the maturity elements into actionable initiatives, it becomes possible to raise the level of architectural maturity within the organization.

8.3.1.3. Elements of Maturity

The maturity model shown in Table 8-26 is characterized by the use of five maturity elements (rows) against the maturity levels described earlier (columns). In practice, the maturity elements in the model may vary slightly from the way they are shown here, but in essence they will boil down to the use of the themes shown in this example.

A remarkably common maturity element is that of assembling an architecture team. While defining and tracking roles and responsibilities is a critical part of *Architecture Governance*, assembling an architecture team is not a stand-alone maturity element.

With recurring regularity, I have seen the inclusion of the architecture team element in a maturity model. In the situation I outlined earlier, where an organization starts to work with architecture, you are often the first (and for a long time the only) architect. Building an architecture team is then not very realistic.

In practice, several roles within the organization are involved in the development of an Enterprise Architecture. The composition of these roles varies.

I have seen compositions of architects, information managers, business analysts, and program managers. Pay close attention to the difference between architecture team members and stakeholders.

If a mixed architecture team is envisioned, it may have a place in the maturity model, but as an item under the Architecture Governance maturity element.

Provide clear definitions of the roles to be used. Use the definitions to determine what is expected of the different roles on the team.

Roles and responsibilities can be included in the context of Architecture Governance. By shifting the focus from the composition of an architecture team to roles and responsibilities, more interpretation is given to what is needed to evolve the architecture capability.

In addition to roles and responsibilities, several additional topics can be identified [25] that can be included in a maturity model. Each of these topics is a useful addition on its own. However, the more elements that are included, the less readable the model becomes. Again, the advice is to start small. If necessary, additional elements can be considered for inclusion in the model in the future.

What can help determine which maturity elements to include in the maturity model is to look at the stages and steps as described in the Enterprise Architecture Implementation Wheel (Figure 8-1). The named steps in the wheel, outside of Maturity, are Information, Stakeholders, Framework, Strategy, Roadmap, and Measure Progress. The Strategy and Roadmap steps can be combined into a single maturity element. When the themes of these steps are incorporated into the maturity model, a framework is created that can be built upon. The integration of the Implementation Wheel and the maturity model provides a way to track the ongoing maturity of the Enterprise Architecture being implemented.

The maturity model used in this book (Table 8-26) has a format with the following topics.

Strategy and vision: The organization has a clear strategy and vision for architecture development that is closely aligned with the organization's goals. There are clear priorities and guidelines for the development of the architecture.

Stakeholder involvement in the architecture is critical to the success of an Enterprise Architecture implementation. Stakeholders include not only architects, but also administrative roles such as senior (business and IT) management. Project and portfolio management also play an important role in the implementation of an Enterprise Architecture. Ideally, there is support at all levels of the organization for the use of architecture and the adoption of architecture products (e.g., basic principles and models).

The Enterprise Architecture is evaluated on a regular basis and suggestions for improvement or evolution are identified. In this way, the effectiveness of the Enterprise Architecture is continuously improved.

The *Strategy* and *Roadmap* steps from the Enterprise Architecture Implementation Wheel can be used for this maturity element.

Architecture governance: The organization has well-trained, experienced, and competent people responsible for developing the architecture. There are clear roles and responsibilities for the architecture function. These are clearly defined so that the entire organization understands what can and cannot be expected of the architecture capability. This prevents discussions and disagreements about architecture.

Training is organized for senior management so that the management level of the organization has sufficient substantive knowledge of Enterprise Architecture. The architecture discipline is also introduced during the onboarding process of new employees. Awareness programs are used to make employees aware of Enterprise Architecture.

Opportunities for collaboration with other similar organizations are actively sought. Experience and ideas are exchanged to improve and develop the Enterprise Architecture.

The step *Measure progress* from the Enterprise Architecture Implementation Wheel aligns with this maturity element.

Architecture method and process: The organization has standardized processes and methods for developing the architecture.

The architecture process, like any other process, needs to be maintained. This ensures the effectiveness and efficiency of the Enterprise Architecture. Captured metrics can be used proactively to identify and make improvements to the architecture process, framework, or products.

However, the development and implementation of an Enterprise Architecture is not an end in itself. Referring back to the earlier definition of Enterprise Architecture (see Chapter 3), it can be said that an Enterprise Architecture ensures that an organization can implement the necessary initiatives to achieve its intended goals and objectives. This can be seen as the purpose of Enterprise Architecture.

In practice, of course, the use and deployment of architecture can vary. For example, it can be used simply as an information conduit (architecture in support of solution delivery) or as a means to drive individual projects (architecture in support of projects). The ultimate goal of Enterprise Architecture is to be a tool that guides the entire organization in achieving business goals (architecture in support of strategy). The uses of Enterprise Architecture are described in more detail in Chapter 7.

The step *Framework* from the Enterprise Architecture Implementation Wheel applies to this maturity element.

Architecture deliverables: The organization has appropriate tools and technologies to develop, implement, and manage the architecture.

Architecture is not just about creating a set of architecture deliverables (such as frameworks, guidelines, and models). Of course, architecture deliverables are very important to have (not for nothing does stage one (*Document*) of the Enterprise Architecture Implementation Wheel place heavy emphasis on them), but they also need to be used and maintained. Maintaining architecture artifacts means updating them and, if necessary, removing artifacts that are no longer applicable. Active maintenance of architecture artifacts ensures that the architecture is and remains current and functional.

Working with architecture can be supported by the use of architecture tools. These tools must be well suited to the task for which they are used. The integrated use of tools, preferably with repository support, maximizes efficiency and effectiveness. This was discussed in Chapter 6, Section 6.4.

The *Information* step from the Enterprise Architecture Implementation Wheel can be used for this maturity element.

Business alignment: The organization has clear controls and governance for architecture development, including measurable performance indicators and quality standards.

The ideal implementation of an Enterprise Architecture is characterized by its use in support of strategy. Simply stating that projects must conform to the architecture is generally not enough. Ultimately, it is up to the organization to decide how to use an Enterprise Architecture (and that may mean using it to manage the portfolio, some individual projects, or even occasionally to achieve specific solutions).

The evolution of an Enterprise Architecture and its alignment with the organization requires regular coordination with various stakeholders. Stakeholders such as senior management, information and project managers, and subject matter experts should be involved. For the architecture process to run smoothly, recurring and regular consultation with stakeholders is essential.

It is necessary to create and increase awareness of the Enterprise Architecture. This introduces the organization to the use and application of architecture concepts and processes. Working with or within the established architecture frameworks (the basic principles) can provide the structure the organization is looking for.

The *Stakeholders* step from the Enterprise Architecture Implementation Wheel is related to this maturity element.

Using the stages from the Implementation Wheel, it is possible to determine where the organization is in terms of architecture maturity. Which issues are well addressed? What issues need additional attention? By checking whether or not the items in the maturity model are satisfied, the current level per maturity element can be determined. Note that if not all of the elements for each level are satisfied, then that level is not applicable, and the previous level applies.

One way to visualize the current level of architectural maturity is to color the topics that are in order or realized (see Table 8-27). A similar approach can be used to visualize the desired level.

Table 8-27. *Colored maturity model showing the current architecture maturity level*

	Ad hoc	Repeatable	Defined	Managed	Optimal
Strategy and vision					
Architecture governance					
Architecture method and process					
Architecture deliverables					
Business alignment					

8.3.1.4. Current and Desired Level

After determining the *current* level of maturity, it is important to clarify what the *desired* level should be. The first step is to determine where the organization is now; what level of maturity the organization has reached. By asking questions regarding the elements of the maturity model, the current maturity level can be determined.

For example, ask whether architecture activities are done on an ad hoc basis or formally initiated. In the former case, it is immediately clear that *Strategy and vision* are at the first level.

Table 8-28. *Example maturity level Strategy and vision*

	Ad hoc	Repeatable	Defined	Managed	Optimal
Strategy and vision	Architecture activities are not formally initiated and happen ad hoc	EA tasks, activities, and required resources are identified	EA activities are implemented according to the established plan	The organization records metrics to measure progress in developing the EA	Action plans are proactively implemented to increase EA effectiveness based on measured data

Another example of a question that could be asked is whether architecture is integrated into the strategic planning of the organization. If this is the case, then the *Architecture method and process* is at level 3. In some cases, further questions are needed. What is the evidence that architecture activities are formally initiated? What examples can be given to show that architecture is actually integrated into strategic planning? It is very easy to answer that everything is in order and under control. Further questioning provides the opportunity to uncover the actual state of affairs.

Table 8-29. *Example maturity level Architecture method and process*

	Ad hoc	Repeatable	Defined	Managed	Optimal
Architecture method and process	Architecture processes are ad hoc and inconsistent	The architecture method is beginning to be reused to capture crucial EA information	EA is integrated into strategic planning	EA is used to guide organizational development	Captured metrics are used to proactively identify and make improvements to EA processes, the EA framework, and/or architecture products

When introducing and implementing Enterprise Architecture in an organization, it is advisable to set a concrete goal in terms of achieving a certain level of maturity. Of course, it is great to be able to say that the organization is at level 5 after a few years of effort, but the question is whether this is realistic and effective enough.

It is wise to work in small steps. Even with small steps, an organization moves forward and the results are visible. Therefore, set the next (or possibly subsequent) level as the goal, counting from the current maturity level. If an organization is at level 1, then the next level to aim for is level 2. If an organization has some things well in place and is somewhere between level 1 and level 2, then the focus can be on achieving level 3.

To get from the current level to the desired level, activities should be performed as described in the maturity model. Look at the topics and activities that need to be implemented according to the target level (see Appendix B: Example Maturity Model for a comprehensive model). Ensure that these topics are reflected in the roadmap for the evolution of the Enterprise Architecture.

One of the main reasons for wanting to achieve an acceptable level of maturity is compliance. Specifically, compliance with laws and regulations. In fact, many organizations are bound by laws and regulations. They are audited on a regular basis. At such times, the organization must be able to demonstrate that it has its affairs in order and is in the process of complying with applicable regulations.

The use of an architecture maturity model makes it possible to meet the requirement to demonstrate compliance. In particular, capturing the essentials ensures that sufficient evidence can be provided to auditors to demonstrate compliance with applicable laws and regulations. The maturity elements that address data capture are therefore critical.

8.3.2. Framework

Table 8-30. *Deliverables of stage two – Define/Framework*

Deliverable	Description
Principles Catalog	Provides an overview of the basic principles

Frameworks can mean several things. In the context of this chapter, a framework deals with basic (or core) principles, requirements, and standards. The second topic from the second stage of the Enterprise Architecture Implementation Wheel deals with this type of framework to be developed. The choice of which architecture framework to use is beyond the scope of this book.

Most organizations have a vision and a mission, elaborate or not. Sometimes an organization is even more advanced and has a strategy in the form of elaborated drivers. This is a good starting point for a framework.

Some time ago, I had the pleasure of sitting down with a group of knowledgeable people for the purpose of establishing basic principles for an organization.

We began the session by taping the brown paper to the wall. The organization was then divided into five domains according to an interoperability model. This interoperability model is characterized by dividing an organization not into the usual three architectural domains (business, information/application, and technology), but into five domains. The business architecture domain is divided into two separate domains (organizational and process-oriented), and the information/application domain is divided into business and information objects on the one hand, and a separate application domain on the other. A total of five domains (see also Chapter 4).

For each domain, my teammates and I tried to identify the key focus areas and activities that the organization was working on, or should be working on, based on the organization's strategy. We then tried to identify the essence of each of these activities. Taken together, this resulted in the creation of the first basic principle.

Each domain that we drew on the brown paper was eventually covered with the sticky notes, and the common denominator of each domain was determined. This eventually led to four basic principles in total, because the application and technology domains together lead to the same principle.

The principles were expressed as succinctly as possible. Not whole sentences, but short and concise and really focused on the essence of the principles. What also helped a lot was translating them into the language that the organization speaks. So not *process-oriented collaboration*, but a *unified way of working*. Process-oriented collaboration is what you can achieve by working in a unified manner. Sometimes the devil really is in the details.

One of the most common mistakes people make when writing principles is thinking that because a phrase is in the imperative, it is automatically a principle. I often see phrases like *cloud first*[5] or *information has an owner*. These are not principles. At best, they are requirements or even standards. And standards are derived from requirements, which are derived from principles. The whole idea behind principles is that they are close to the business goals to be achieved. They can then be further specified and detailed by requirements, supplemented by standards if necessary.

The four basic principles were soon established and provided a starting point for the organization to conduct its activities in a more structured and focused manner.

The four basic principles were soon after established and marked the starting point for the organization to implement its activities in a more structured and determined manner.

Sections 8.3.2.2 through 8.3.2.4 discuss the development of basic principles, requirements, and standards. The structure of the principles, requirements, and standards can be visualized using a Framework Pyramid.

---

[5] *Cloud first* may actually be a principle if the organization is to provide IT services to its customers.

8.3.2.1. Framework Pyramid

At the top of the pyramid are the basic principles. The middle layer represents the requirements, and the base of the pyramid represents the standards. An initial insight provided by a Framework Pyramid relates to the numbers to be used for the framework concepts. In Figure 8-15, it is easy to see that the top of the pyramid is relatively small. This is a direct reflection of the recommended number of basic principles. Again, less is more. The layer below, that of requirements, is already somewhat wider, indicating that there can be more requirements than basic principles. The bottom layer, where the standards are, is the broadest layer. This means that there are more standards than basic principles and requirements.

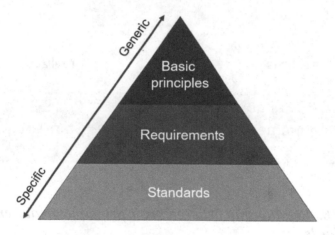

Figure 8-15. *Framework Pyramid*

A second insight is that reading from top to bottom, the degree of specificity increases as you go down. A requirement is more detailed than a principle, and a standard is much more specific than a requirement.

Aside from the fact that requirements are more detailed than principles, there is another difference between the two concepts. Principles are directive (and therefore not mandatory), while requirements can be seen as prescriptive (and indeed mandatory). The wording of the concepts also plays an important role. This is the distinction between *generic* properties and *specific* properties. A principle states a property without detail and at a high level (generic). A requirement makes this generic property specific. For example, a principle might state that laws and regulations must be followed. The principle does not specify which laws and regulations. A requirement specifies this. Finally, a standard is simply the result of a broad specification of a requirement.

The relationship between basic principles, requirements, and standards is shown in Figure 8-16.

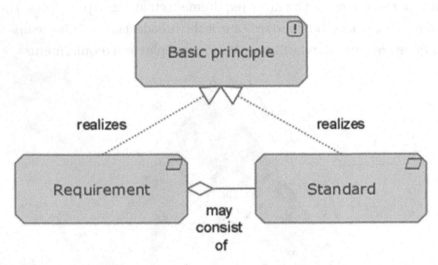

Figure 8-16. *Relationship between basic principles, requirements, and standards*

When the elements shown in Figure 8-16 are plotted on the Framework Pyramid (Figure 8-15), it can be seen that the middle layer, requirements, can be translated into the architecture element requirement. In the bottom layer of the pyramid, standards are visualized using the same element. This is because the ArchiMate modeling language does not distinguish between requirements and standards. Both concepts are represented by the element requirement (see also Chapter 6, Section 6.2.1).

8.3.2.2. Basic Principles

Basic principles are similar to assumptions that are made about general descriptions of how a system works. The word principle comes from the Latin word *principium,* which means *beginning* and *foundation.* Here you can clearly see the relationship to what IEEE 1471 [6] indicates in its definition of a architecture.

[Architecture consists of] *fundamental concepts* or properties of a system in its environment embodied in its elements, relationships, and in the *principles* of its design and evolution [6].

Enterprise Architecture principles often give meaning to the core parameters of the whole. They give meaning to the extent to which systems are sourced, the degree of integration, centralization, and specialization of systems, and the degree of innovation the organization intends to pursue.

The TOGAF Standard defines principles as follows.

Principles are general rules and guidelines, intended to be enduring and seldom amended, that inform and support the way in which an organization sets about fulfilling its mission [22].

The examples provided in the TOGAF Standard resemble high-level and organization-wide guidelines. In this form, principles are similar to the constitution of a country. They have a high level of abstraction and serve as a kind of guiding light that can be used to give further direction and interpretation to their application and use. They are highly influential and strategic in nature. They are carefully designed to fit the organization and its business model. Like a constitution, these principles change little or nothing and have a strong binding character. The high-level or basic principles are based on business goals and objectives [9].

Basic principles are used to establish high-level frameworks that can be applied to all types of topics and issues facing an organization. They serve as tools to provide structure and direction to a wide variety of issues. Basic principles can be thought of as guardrails on a highway. They indicate that you should drive within the guardrails. Often they go so far as to indicate that you should drive from A to B. What the principles do not do is specify how fast you should (or should not) drive, what vehicle you should use, or what requirements the vehicle should meet. That level of detail is left to requirements and standards.

Basic principles, as explained in Section 8.3.2.1, form the top of the Framework Pyramid. This means that there should not be hundreds of principles. An average of four or five is more than sufficient. The key is to work toward the suggested number. If, despite your best efforts, more than the suggested four or five basic principles have been developed, it is still advisable to take another look at the framework that has been established. If possible, try to combine or simplify topics so that the suggested four or five principles remain.

The reason for keeping the number of principles small has to do with the ramifications from principle to requirement and from requirement to standard. Assuming that each basic principle can easily have three requirements, and that each requirement may have about five standards, this results in sixty ($4 \cdot 3 \cdot 5 = 60$) standards with four basic principles. If six basic principles are developed, then with the same number of requirements and standards, this can easily result in a total of ninety ($6 \cdot 3 \cdot 5 = 90$) standards.

The number of standards can grow very quickly. And although standards can help an organization shape the contours to be used, too many standards actually backfire. Too many standards work too restrictively, because too many standards take away any freedom of movement. Keeping the number of basic principles small is essential to the application of an appropriate framework.

There are several factors that influence or determine the establishment of principles [26]:

- The organization's mission and vision, plans, and organizational structure.

- The organization's strategic goals and intended objectives.

- External influences, such as market forces, new developments, emerging trends, existing and future laws and regulations.

- The current environment (and state) of information systems, policies, and procedures.

Establishing good principles depends heavily on following the definition. ArchiMate defines a principle as follows.

A principle represents a statement of intent defining a general property that applies to any system in a certain context in the architecture [12].

The definition refers to a *system*. This system should be seen as referring to a business actor, a business process, a business object, an application component, or a data object. All of these elements are considered *systems*. A principle expresses an intent to name a property of one of the above elements. As an example, a basic principle may state that an unambiguous way of working should be applied to all activities that an organization undertakes and performs. This unambiguous way of working refers to the handling and execution of business processes, one of the *systems* listed in the ArchiMate definition.

A second example could be to store information once and use it more often. This basic principle says something about the information concept that must be used to satisfy the basic principle. So in this second example, the term system refers to an information concept.

In situations where I need to explain the establishment and use of basic principles, I always like to use the example of the fictional organization Lemon-A-de (see also Chapter 10). This company sells lemonade and wants to become the market leader.

One of the most important basics for Lemon-A-de is to use quality limes. In fact, the fruit they use is essential to making quality lemonade.

This is how the basic principle *use only A-brand limes* was born.

The *system* mentioned in the ArchiMate definition in this example refers to a *business object* (the limes). The *quality of the fruit* is the *property* assigned to the system, in this example the limes.

To arrive at a set of basic principles, it is important to look at the organization as a whole. By asking a few simple questions, it should be possible to get to the heart of what is important to the organization:

- What is the organization on earth for?
- What does the organization really want to accomplish?
- What drives the organization to do what it does every day?
- What is most important to the organization (what processes and applications)?
- What internal and external factors impact the organization?

In fact, these are pretty much the same questions that can be asked to arrive at goals and their associated objectives. The questions (and answers) can also be used to establish basic principles.

When establishing the basics, it is important to avoid going into too much detail. Make sure that there is a clear description of the principles and their requirements. Give each principle a name, an explanation, a rationale, and implications. The best results are achieved by describing the principles and requirements in the language of the organization. Stay away from the more static language of Enterprise Architecture, and use the language of the organization. Describe the principles and requirements in a way that everyone in the organization can read and understand.

To ensure adoption of the principles, it is advisable to involve stakeholders in the process of defining the principles. This could be achieved by organizing workshops in which stakeholders can participate. By actively involving stakeholders in the process, the principles become more of a collaborative effort rather than something that feels imposed.

A basic principle always consists of the following components:

Name: The name of the principle represents its essence. Choose a name that is easy to remember and avoid including details. For example, never refer to specific technologies, platforms, products, or specific laws and regulations. Avoid ambiguous words.

Explanation: Provide a clear (short) explanation of the principle. Summarize the meaning in one sentence.

Rationale: The rationale presents the benefits of applying the principle. It uses the language of the organization.

Implications: Implications indicate what is needed to implement or be able to apply the basic principle. For example, consider the resources or costs required. The impact of applying the principle needs to be made clear.

In addition to the above, the TOGAF standard provides several other criteria [26] for establishing basic principles. For example, the principles must be sufficiently complete to apply to any situation, and, above all, they must be understandable. The terms *consistent* and *stable* are mentioned in the architecture framework and should also apply to the principles.

In many cases, an organization depends on a few essential things to achieve its goals. These include the delivery of products and/or services, the delivery of products and/or services according to a consistent way of working, the efficient use of information, and compliance with applicable laws and regulations.

The above essentials can be easily translated into the following four basic principles:

Comply with laws and regulations: To comply with laws and regulations, relevant laws and regulations are considered in the development, procurement, and design of systems, products, and services.

Unambiguous ways of working: Consistent ways of performing tasks and activities are used. The best way of working is chosen so that work is done more efficiently. This ensures that information management is under control.

Store information once and use it more often: Used information is recorded once, and in one place so it can be used more often. Information is available from a single source.

Standard products and services: Off-the-shelf applications and IT systems are used as much as possible. Products and services are selected based on the functionality required for the task.

Of course, not every organization is the same. Therefore, not all of the above principles can be applied without modification. For this reason, the above set of four basic principles is intended as an illustration or starting point.

Introducing basic principles into the organization will initially be met with resistance. This is because people will feel restricted in their freedom to do their daily work. However, the basic principles are not meant to hinder people in their work. They are there to structure the way processes are handled, to guarantee the availability of information and systems, and to ensure that the organization is sufficiently compliant with laws and regulations. One way – and there are several ways – to increase the adoption of the basic principles is to make the introduction as attractive as possible.

Section 8.2.2.5 briefly mentioned enlisting the help of departments such as communications and graphic design. The great advantage of using these auxiliaries is that they speak the language of the organization like no other. Again, the importance of uniformity of language is evident.

At one point, when I wanted to introduce a set of basic principles to an organization where I was working, I called in the graphic design department. We worked together to describe the four basic principles in the language of the organization. This meant paying attention to word choice and sentence structure, as well as delivering the message in a one-liner that was as short as possible and, above all, understandable.

We also used icons that captured the essence of the principles. The association of the icon with the one-liner of the basic principle resulted in it being well remembered by employees.

By leveraging the knowledge and expertise of departments such as communications and graphic design, I was able to bring the basic principles to life for employees. This ensured that the organization quickly recognized and adopted the principles.

8.3.2.3. Requirements

Further specifying basic principles gives more direction to what the organization has or should have in mind. For example, consider the principle of complying with laws and regulations. This principle does not specify the exact laws and regulations. A requirement can provide more detail by identifying specific laws and regulations. A requirement also indicates what additional conditions are imposed. A standard goes one level deeper. For example, consider securing access to certain information with a multi-factor authentication solution. Looking more closely at this example, the part about securing access to certain information is the actual requirement, while the part that mentions using a multi-factor authentication solution is the standard to be used.

To explain exactly what a requirement is, it is necessary to start with initiatives. The implementation of one or more initiatives ultimately realizes the organization's goals and objectives (Section 8.3.3 discusses goals, objectives, and initiatives in more detail). These initiatives can be captured in a project plan or, if of a larger scope, in a program plan. A requirement indicates the changes needed to a new or existing situation, environment, process, or system within the context of the initiative. A requirement indicates what is needed to achieve the intended change.

ArchiMate offers the following definition of a requirement.

A requirement represents a statement of need defining a property that applies to a specific system as described by the architecture [12].

Unlike a requirement, a goal articulates a desired end result in a high-level way. For example, consider *Improve portfolio management*. The word *improve* leaves a lot to the imagination. As soon as the meaning of the goal is detailed enough that it can be realized by a person or a system, we talk about a requirement. For example, the goal *Improve portfolio management* might have the following two requirements:

- Assign a liaison to each department.

- Implement an online portfolio management tool.

Both requirements further specify the goal to be achieved. The first requirement is executable by a person, the second by a software application (a system). Requirements form the binding framework.

By asking a series of questions, requirements can be identified:

- Can the basic principles be further specified?

- What direction (what detail) can be given to the stated basic principle?

- What needs to be clearly defined (e.g., because of laws and regulations)?

- How should situations or information systems be handled?

The set of requirements to be prepared varies in size and from initiative to initiative. Sometimes there are initiatives that can get by with just a few requirements. Other situations require a more comprehensive set. What helps is to provide the basic principles with *generic requirements*. That is, a set of requirements that provides enough detail, but also leaves room for use in a variety of initiatives.

An example of such a requirement is *to store information in a central location*. This requirement states that there must be a central location for storing information, but it does not specify what that location should look like. This is the space that is being talked about. Another example is a requirement that states that the *purchase of cloud services is preferred over locally installed software*. This reiterates the basic principle of using off-the-shelf products and services. However, by not specifying which cloud services are included and which are not, it leaves enough room for the requirement to be applied to different initiatives.

A good rule of thumb when writing requirements is to have no more than four or five requirements per basic principle. Of course, six requirements are not immediately a problem, but ten requirements (or more) per principle will quickly become confusing. Always ask yourself whether a written requirement is specific to a particular project or program, or whether it is general enough to fit within a principle. The more specific requirements should not be part of the more general requirements related to the principles.

8.3.2.4. Standards

Sections 8.3.2.2 and 8.3.2.3 discussed basic principles and requirements. These two elements form the top two layers of the Framework Pyramid (Figure 8-15). Standards are at the bottom of the Framework Pyramid and are similar to very detailed requirements. They indicate a clear preference, a standard.

Standards are created in a number of ways. The first and most common way is to write a very detailed requirement. An example used earlier (see Chapter 6, Section 6.4.1.3) shows that the use of an MFA solution can be a standard, which is formed by a requirement as a derivative of a basic principle. A requirement says something about the *application* of MFA from a legal and regulatory perspective, while a standard specifies the *final form*. Figure 8-17 illustrates the creation of a standard.

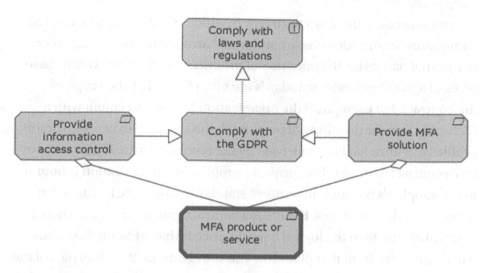

Figure 8-17. *Example of a standard*

A second way to create a standard is through the use of best practices. Market research can help determine the most appropriate standard. Conducting a survey of the use of solutions at similar institutions or companies can also help determine the most appropriate standards.

For example, it is very common in the healthcare industry to look at other hospitals and find out what (off-the-shelf) solutions they are using.

If the experience with a particular product or service is good, word spreads quickly to other hospitals. This was the case with an MFA solution, for example.

In the region where I worked, there were a number of hospitals using a particular MFA solution. Their experience was so good that I decided to implement a similar solution for the hospital where I worked.

The solution used in the region became a widely used standard.

In some cases, there is a third way in which standards can be created. Sometimes organizations have contractual arrangements with suppliers or external parties for the purchase of products and services. When these types of agreements exist, standards are often limited by the scope of the contract. For example, if the organization has an agreement with a recruiting firm for the hiring of personnel, the standard to be used for job profiles will most likely be one used by the recruiting firm. If the company has a contract with an office furniture supplier, the organization is bound to the supplier's products in terms of standards. The same is true when purchasing cloud services. If there is a contract that provides a particular cloud platform, then the logical consequence is that additional services will be provided from that platform. The standards are therefore part of the services offered.

For the Enterprise Architect, this third way of creating standards is the least comfortable. From an Enterprise Architecture perspective, there is no room for maneuver in the formulation of standards. A number of frameworks are already determined by the existing contractual agreements, beyond the influence and strategic view of the Enterprise Architecture.

Standards created by the Enterprise Architect or imposed by contractual agreements reside in the Architecture Repository. A special part of the repository is the Standards Library. This library contains the standards to which the Enterprise Architecture must conform. The Standards Library consists of business standards, information standards, data and application standards, and technology standards. Some examples of standards that may appear in the library include:

- Specific standards for a particular industry (e.g., healthcare or government).

- Selected vendor products and services (think of a specific cloud platform).

- Established information sets (e.g., care status information in terms of regional bed utilization).

- Specific services or products already used by the organization (e.g., use of a customer relationship management system to capture customer information).

- Well-defined job profiles used by a recruiting firm.

Each domain in the architecture has standards. For example, the *business domain* includes *business roles* such as nurse, accountant, air traffic controller, or auto mechanic. These roles are used to assign responsibilities or a salary. Business roles are also used to grant access to information or applications, or to physical rooms in a building. In addition to business roles, *business actors* can also be included in a standard. This could involve specific suppliers, as these are also business actors and can therefore be included in the Standards Library.

In the *information domain*, certain *information concepts* can be used to provide context to raw data. One example is regional hospital bed occupancy rates. The raw data (records) show the number of beds in use at different hospitals. The Bed Occupancy information concept provides context to the data and can therefore be used as a standard.

The *data domain* is the architecture domain where *application interfaces* such as APIs are used. The use of API interfaces can be made a standard when it comes to requesting information. The structure or composition of a *data object* (record) can also serve as a standard. The combination of name, address, and city is an example of a commonly used standard.

Standards are also used in the *application domain*. Consider, for example, the most widely used word processor, MS Word. The use of a standard does not mean that other *applications* with similar functionality cannot or should not exist in an organization. A good example of two applications that both provide document creation functionality are the aforementioned word processor and Adobe Acrobat. In most organizations, both Word and PDF documents are used.

Finally, there is the *technology domain*. This is the architecture domain most often associated with the word standard. Perhaps this is because nine times out of ten, a standard is used to describe a well-defined *technical solution*. One of the best-known standards is the choice of operating system. A particular version of an operating system can also become a standard. Physical or virtual hardware is also often defined as a standard.

There is no general rule for determining whether one standard is more applicable than another. When designing and creating standards, it is important to look at your own organization. What works best for the organization? What is used most often? What provides the most value to the company? Label those products or solutions as standards and store them in the Architecture Repository. Most standards are elevated to architecture building blocks, making them reusable.

8.3.3. Strategy

Table 8-31. *Deliverables of stage two – Define/Strategy*

Deliverable	Description
Strategy/Goal Matrix	Cross-mapping of drivers and goals
Goal/Objective Matrix	Cross-mapping of goals and objectives
Objective/Initiative Matrix	Cross-mapping of objectives and initiatives

Creating a business strategy has long been recognized as one of the most important ways to allocate resources within an organization to achieve specific goals. A strategy is then implemented to achieve these goals and often includes the processes by which the strategy is created. It also includes initiatives for implementing the strategy and techniques for controlling and monitoring the initial implementation. Strategy formulation addresses aspects of organizational motivation such as vision, mission, and goals. Strategy builds on an organization's drivers to provide an actionable path for achieving some or all of its goals.

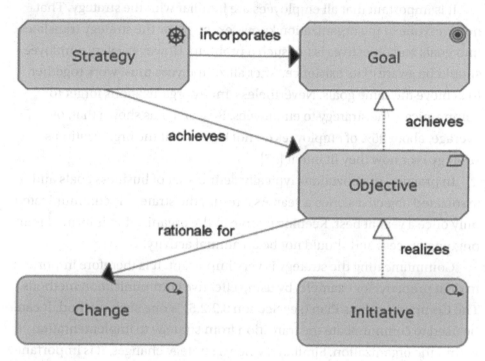

Figure 8-18. *Relationship between strategy, goals, objectives, and initiatives*

An organization's strategy is constantly evolving. This is driven by internal and external factors that influence an organization's strategy. Therefore, it is only logical to review the strategy on an annual basis to see if the motivations and goals are still appropriate for the time and environment in which the organization finds itself. If the market has changed, the strategy may need to change with it.

Although organizations generally agree that the ability to execute a strategy is essential to achieving goals, by no means do all organizations properly translate a strategy into execution. One of the most glaring failures is the lack of communication of strategy to the people in the organization. Yet, this is one of the most important factors for successful strategy implementation.

It is important that all employees are familiar with the strategy. That not everyone in the organization knows exactly how the strategy translates into goals and objectives is not such a problem. However, every employee should be aware of its existence. After all, employees must work together to achieve the same goals. Nevertheless, many organizations forget to communicate the strategy to employees. Research has shown that, on average, about 95% of employees do not know what the organization's strategy is or how they fit into it [27].

In practice, organizations typically define a set of business goals and associated objectives once a year. As a result, the strategy is communicated only once a year at best. Keeping people in the organization informed is an ongoing process and should not be an annual activity.

Communicating the strategy is very important. It is therefore important to do it properly, for example, by using effective communication methods. The Communications Plan (see Section 8.2.2.5) is one such method. It can be used to communicate the transition from strategy to implementation within the organization. Similarly, when a strategy changes, it is important to communicate the changes appropriately to the internal organization. Changes need to be brought to the attention of the organization on an ongoing basis with some form of regularity.

Almost every organization has a strategy. However, the form in which such a strategy exists varies greatly from organization to organization. Some organizations will have elaborated it more than others, but in nine out of ten cases a strategy is present. The trick in translating strategy into execution is to help the organization walk the strategic path as much as possible.

Establishing, or sometimes first distilling, drivers, goals, and objectives is one of the activities an Enterprise Architect must perform to arrive at initiatives that will help the organization achieve its strategic goals.

In my experience, one organization did have a strategy, but it was described in a very narrative way. The strategy was about 20 pages of what the organization stood for and what the focus areas were for the next three to five years.

In order to translate that strategy into concrete goals and measurable objectives, I had to organize several long sessions with the members of the board of directors, and the various management teams to translate the large chunks of text from the articulation of the strategy into goals and objectives. The more descriptions of intended objectives there are in a strategic agenda, the more difficult it is to translate them into goals.

Identifying and distilling the goals of the 20-page strategy was challenging, to say the least. It took many hours to match related objectives to the right goals. This had everything to do with the fact that people in the organization were not used to naming measurable and time-bound goals. It also felt overwhelming and oppressive to many.

By actually making the goals to be achieved measurable and putting a deadline on them, a number of managers felt that they could be held accountable in very specific ways if the intended results were not achieved. People did not see the implementation of the strategy as something positive, but rather as something very negative. Again, it took many conversations to correct this image.

Virtually all architecture frameworks state that establishing (or distilling) goals and objectives is one of the first steps in developing an Enterprise Architecture. In practice, however, this happens later in the process. Admittedly, in an ideal world, establishing goals and objectives would be one of the first activities. After all, everything that follows depends on or is related to those goals and objectives. But practice is often more unruly. Therefore, the Enterprise Architecture Implementation Wheel (Figure 8-1) takes a different approach and sequence. The strategy, drivers, goals, objectives, and initiatives are defined in the second stage (*Define*).

8.3.3.1. Drivers

Drivers are motivating elements. They are the areas of focus for an organization that show where it is going in the future. Drivers are strategic in nature and describe the state or condition that motivates an organization to define its goals and make the changes or adjustments necessary to achieve them.

In the recent past, I worked for an organization where the application of language consistency was a relatively unknown concept.

This organization had a desire to get a better handle on the execution of the strategic agenda. However, when it came to translating that into operations, things often went awry.

I did a quick survey of how people were translating strategy and found that there were several programs that were doing (parts of) the translation from strategy to execution. I also noticed that different terms were being used for the same topics.

In my research, I came across the terms *strategic spearheads*, *strategic agenda*, *amplifiers*, *accelerators*, and *strategic themes*. They all refer to or represent what we in architecture call drivers.

Because there were so many different initiatives, all trying to achieve the same goal, it was not clear to the organization which ones to follow. They could not see the forest for the many trees because each of the initiatives had its own interpretation of what was meant by the term drivers.

I introduced the concept of consistent language by including it as a requirement in one of the basic principles I developed for the organization. The requirement for consistency of language reduced the variety of names for the same thing to a single definition.

Only when the organization got to the point where when they talked about a driver, they really meant a driver, was it possible to translate the strategy into concrete goals and objectives.

Drivers are external or internal conditions, events, or trends that create the need for an organization to initiate or adapt its architecture to achieve specific results. They are critical to ensuring that the Enterprise Architecture is strategically aligned with the organization's goals and objectives. By understanding the drivers, architects can tailor the architecture to address the specific challenges and opportunities presented by those drivers.

When an Enterprise Architect can articulate how the architecture addresses the various drivers, it becomes easier to gain stakeholder support and demonstrate the business value of proposed architectural changes. Drivers provide the rationale for architectural decisions and help identify the most important requirements that the architecture must meet. By analyzing the drivers, the architect can determine the specific capabilities and features that the architecture should have to meet the needs of the organization.

Drivers are essential for managing changes to the architecture. As drivers change or new drivers emerge, the architect must assess their impact on the architecture and adapt accordingly. By understanding the drivers, architects can plan for change, manage stakeholder expectations, and ensure a smooth transition during implementation. By analyzing drivers, architects can identify potential risks that could affect the success of the architecture initiative. They can then develop risk mitigation strategies to proactively address these concerns.

Drivers play a critical role in architecture initiatives. They provide the context and justification for investing in specific architectural changes, which is critical to gaining buy-in and funding for projects. Driver analysis is an ongoing activity in Enterprise Architecture. As the organization evolves and new drivers emerge, architects must assess their relevance and adjust the architecture to remain aligned with the strategic direction of the business.

The driver concept helps the Enterprise Architect understand the factors that necessitate changes to the organization's architecture. By considering these drivers, the architect can make informed decisions, prioritize efforts, and ensure that the architecture is responsive to the organization's strategic goals and the evolving business landscape.

When an organization begins to work with architecture, it is wise to examine whether drivers are already being used. Drivers may be wrapped up in extensive language that the organization has used to describe its strategic direction. If so, distill the drivers from the text and refine them as necessary.

In addition to being used to express an organization's motivation to achieve its goals, drivers are also used in the context of stakeholders. The drivers associated with a stakeholder are often referred to as the stakeholder's concerns. Freely translated, this *means something that the stakeholder's attention is focused on*. Stakeholder concerns are defined in the TOGAF standard as:

An interest in a system that is relevant to one or more of its stakeholders. Concerns may relate to any aspect of the system's operation, development or operation, including considerations such as performance, reliability, safety, distribution and evolvability and may determine the acceptability of the system [1].

Examples of internal drivers include *appropriate care, customer satisfaction,* and *profitability.* Drivers of change can also be external to the organization (e.g., economic changes or changing legislation). A driver is not always associated with a stakeholder.

When formulating drivers, a noun is preferred. A good definition is essential when formulating drivers. Drivers must be described very clearly and without differences of interpretation. Including a clearly explainable definition is an absolute must.

A driver represents an external or internal condition that motivates an organization to define its goals and implement the changes necessary to achieve them [12].

If an organization's motivations are not sufficiently clear, or if it proves unexpectedly difficult to distill them from the available documents, the following questions can be asked to find out:

- What is the organization on earth for?

- What drives the organization to do what it does every day?

- What focus areas motivate the organization?

Defining the drivers is an activity that must be done at the highest level of the organization. There must be consensus on what motivates the organization to achieve its goals, and this can only happen if it is defined at the board or executive level. Having a sponsor at this level in the organization is essential. Without a supported strategy, the goals and objectives that are subsequently formulated and defined are nothing more than loose sand.

8.3.3.2. Goals

Table 8-32. *Deliverables of the focus area Goals*

Deliverable	Description
Strategy/Goal Matrix	Cross-mapping of drivers and goals

The development of goals is critical for defining strategic objectives, guiding architectural decisions, and ensuring alignment between business needs and IT solutions. Goals provide a basis for prioritizing efforts, measuring success, and maintaining focus on achieving desired outcomes for the organization. By using goals effectively, the Enterprise Architect can create well-supported and effective architectures that drive the organization toward its strategic goals and long-term success.

A goal is a fundamental concept used to represent the desired outcome or objective that an organization seeks to achieve. Goals in Enterprise Architecture help define the strategic intent of the organization and provide a clear direction for the development of the architecture. They are essential for ensuring that the Enterprise Architecture is aligned with the overall strategic goals of the organization. By understanding the goals, the Enterprise Architect can design an architecture that supports and contributes to the achievement of these goals.

Goals serve as the basis for eliciting architectural requirements. By understanding the desired outcomes, architects can identify the capabilities and features that the architecture must have to meet the needs of the organization. Goals provide the rationale for architectural decisions. When architects can tie their decisions to specific goals, it becomes easier to gain stakeholder support and demonstrate the business value of proposed architectural changes.

Goals are used to measure the performance and success of the architecture. Architects can track progress toward goals and evaluate the effectiveness of the architecture in achieving desired outcomes. Goals play a critical role in building the business case for architecture initiatives. They provide the context and justification for investing in specific architectural changes, which is critical to gaining approval and funding for projects.

So, a goal can be seen as an achievable dot on the horizon. A goal should be achievable within three to five years. This makes a goal a long-term outcome. Goals are directly related to the strategic drivers of the organization.

A goal represents a high-level statement of intent, direction, or desired end state for an organization and its stakeholders [12].

When formulating goals, try to set them using the SMART method. This method is based on assigning about five values to a goal to make it concrete. SMART stands for Specific, Measurable, Assignable, Realistic, Time-related. It provides criteria to help formulate goals and objectives [28].

Table 8-33. *SMART definition*

Value	Description
Specific	Target a specific area for improvement
Measurable	Quantify or at least suggest an indicator of progress
Assignable	Specify who will do it
Realistic	State what results can realistically be achieved, given available resources
Time-bound	Specify when the result(s) can be achieved

Over the years, several variations of the SMART method have emerged. For example, *Achievable* is often used instead of *Assignable*, and *Realistic* is used instead of *Relevant*.

The application of the SMART method is as follows. First, a goal is formulated using the value *Specific*. A specific area of interest and improvement is used to define the goal. In this example, the production of lemonade is assumed.

Produce the best lemonade there is.

This goal initially sets a high standard without being very concrete. By adding the other values from the SMART method to the stated goal, it becomes more concrete and therefore more achievable. After *Specific*, the value *Measurable* is applied.

Produce at least one bottle of the best lemonade there is per person worldwide.

The additions of "at least one bottle of" and "per person worldwide" create metrics. These can be used to determine whether the goal has been met at any given time. The goal is still not concrete enough and may not be realistic either. Applying the value *Assignable* has no added value for this particular goal. The entire company is involved in achieving the goal. The *Realistic* value, on the other hand, is important to apply to this goal.

Produce at least one bottle of A-class lemonade per inhabitant of the country.

First of all, "the best lemonade there is" has been replaced with "A-class lemonade." It sounds idyllic to be the best, but only a few actually achieve it. Therefore, it is wiser and more realistic to say that an A-class lemonade is being produced. A second change is to replace "worldwide" with "of the country." This again makes the goal much more realistic. Of course, it is good to dare to dream, but starting with both feet on the ground will yield more results. A final application is that of the *Time-bound* value.

By 2030, Lemon-A-de produces at least one bottle of A-class lemonade per inhabitant of the country.

The fictitious company Lemon-A-de (see also Chapter 10) has set itself the goal of producing Class A lemonade by the year 2030 in such a way that it is able to produce at least one bottle of lemonade per inhabitant of the country in which the company is located. By applying the SMART method, a feasible, measurable, and, above all, realistic goal was created.

As the example shows, setting goals is a difficult and sometimes lengthy process. The following questions can help to get a picture of what is really important to an organization:

- What does the organization really want to accomplish?

- When does the organization want to achieve it?

- What is most important to the organization?

- What internal and external factors influence the organization?

- Where does the organization want to be in three to five years?

- How can this be made measurable?

- Is the stated goal realistic enough?

Section 8.3.2.2 described the reason for limiting the number of basic principles, requirements, and standards (the rapid growth in numbers due to the amount of branching). The same reason applies to drivers, goals, and objectives. Therefore, for each driver, formulate no more than three to five goals. Remember that each goal is made up of one or more objectives. For example, if an organization has five drivers, three goals for each driver, and three objectives for each goal, there are easily 45 objectives to achieve. The more drivers and goals an organization defines, the larger the set of objectives will be. As the number of goals increases, the plausibility of actually achieving all of them will greatly decrease. The key is to stay realistic and focused. Determine what is really important to the organization and try not to list every possible goal. A strategy has a focus, a subset of what the organization stands for. A strategy does not include everything an organization does or should do.

In a recent past, I worked for an organization that was unable to formulate goals. Formulating a strategy with a set of drivers was possible, but translating those drivers into concrete goals proved to be quite a task.

By repeatedly sitting down with the board and remaining disciplined in the use of consistent language (a driver is a driver, not a spearhead, amplifier, accelerator, or theme), I was eventually able to identify four drivers that revealed the organization's focus for the next three to five years.

I discussed these drivers extensively with the board to get a good sense of what they meant. Once the definition of each drive was clearly articulated and agreement was reached on the definitions, time was spent determining what the desired end result should be in line with the previously defined drivers.

By asking the organization, "If this is what drives and motivates you, what do you want to accomplish in five years," statements began to emerge that pointed in the direction of the goals. It took several sessions, but eventually we were able to translate what the organization wanted to achieve into concrete, SMART goals.

This was followed by the question of what the desired or intended objective (or objectives) should be for each goal. This exercise went more smoothly as people began to get used to using a consistent language. Objectives were formulated in a relatively short time.

In the end, the organization identified four drivers, each with three goals. For each goal, the decision was made to set five objectives. The roadmap that was later created contained a total of about 60 objectives, divided into a large number of work packages.

In the first stage (*Document*) of the Enterprise Architecture Implementation Wheel, the organization, processes, information concepts, applications, and technology components in use have been mapped and documented. Now, the various architecture deliverables can be used to determine the impact on the organization in relation to the stated goals and intended objectives.

Architecture deliverables in the form of matrices play an important role here. It helps an organization enormously to have a matrix that visualizes the relationship between the established goals on the one hand and the intended objectives on the other. Knowing what needs to be done to achieve the goals is of great value to the organization. Especially when the objectives are enriched with initiatives. In this way, it is possible to specify exactly which activities must be carried out in order to achieve a certain goal. By taking this a step further and linking business processes and business actors, it is possible to show, down to the level of a department (or even a specific business role within a department), what is needed (and by whom) to realize the objectives – and thus the realization of the strategy. Figure 8-19 in Section 8.3.3.4 illustrates the relationship between the above concepts.

Once it is clear what the goals and objectives of the organization are, it is possible to identify their impact on existing processes. In Section 8.2.1.2, reference was made to a business function, *Order Processing*, that appeared to trigger the process of creating an invoice. It turned out that this process was actually part of another business function, *Payment Processing*. Now, if the organization in the example decides to stop offering certain products due to a change in the strategy, this could affect the process that creates the invoices, and thus the business function Payment Processing. Or, if the organization decides to offer the ability to purchase products on account, prompted by the establishment of a new goal, this could affect both the Order Processing and Payment Processing business functions.

Understanding the processes used by the organization is essential to determining the impact of setting goals and objectives during the *Define* stage. This underscores the importance of careful and thorough execution of the *Document* stage of the Enterprise Architecture Implementation Wheel.

Strategy/Goal Matrix

The Strategy/Goal Matrix shows the relationship between the strategic drivers and the organization's goals to be achieved.

Table 8-34. *Strategy/Goal Matrix*

| | Goals | | | | |
	Goal A	Goal B	Goal C	Goal D	Goal E
Strategic drivers					
Driver A	X	X			
Driver B			X		
Driver C				X	X

Actors such as boards of directors or other forms of senior management are typically responsible for achieving business goals. By visualizing the relationship between the elements, a Strategy/Goal Matrix makes it clear where there may be overlapping responsibilities. It is important to use this insight to ensure clarity about where responsibilities should be placed. This avoids finger-pointing in the event of disappointing results.

8.3.3.3. Objectives

Table 8-35. *Deliverables of the focus area Objectives*

Deliverable	Description
Goal/Objective Matrix	Cross-mapping of goals and objectives. Objectives are supported with a clear definition. The definition is formulated using the SMART method

Objectives, like goals, align with the organization's strategy. Also like goals, they are defined in a specific, measurable, achievable, relevant, and time-bound manner. Objectives serve as actionable guidelines that guide architectural decisions, resource allocation, and performance measurement. Objectives provide a more concrete and detailed expression of the broader goals, breaking them down into manageable and achievable components. They serve as actionable targets that guide the organization's efforts in pursuit of its strategic intent.

Objectives help align the Enterprise Architecture with the strategic goals of the organization. By defining specific and measurable objectives, architects can ensure that the architecture is designed to support the achievement of those objectives. They also serve as the basis for eliciting architectural requirements. Architects can identify the capabilities and features needed in the architecture to meet the defined objectives.

Therefore, objectives provide a clear rationale for architectural choices. When the architect can link their choices to specific objectives, it becomes easier to prioritize efforts and make informed decisions that align with the strategic direction of the organization.

Objectives are primarily used to measure the performance and success of the execution of the organization's strategy. However, they can also be used to measure the success and performance of the (implementation of) Enterprise Architecture. The architect can track progress toward the objectives and assess the effectiveness of the architecture in meeting those objectives. The Enterprise Architecture must continually adapt to support the organization's changing objectives.

Setting goals is one of the most difficult parts of formulating a strategy. The objectives must demonstrate that the implementation of the strategic plan is likely to achieve the intended overarching goals. Herein lies an enormous task for senior management.

An objective is a quantitative, actionable and measurable result that defines strategy and achieves a goal [8].

In practice, the formulated objectives are often too focused on concrete actions to be taken. Senior management often thinks from an overly operational perspective. This common situation means that in most cases what the company wants to achieve is lost. The consequences of formulating activities versus a goal-oriented strategic planning approach often result in unclear measures of success. This leads to an inability to determine whether an objective has been achieved and whether an initiative has failed or succeeded. The SMART method described in Section 8.3.3.2 can help to formulate objectives correctly.

Asking senior management the following questions will help to get a clear picture of the objectives that need to be defined to achieve the organization's goals:

- What exactly must the organization do to achieve its goals?

- What happens if the organization doesn't?

- What (actionable) steps need to be taken?

- Can the steps be clearly defined and made SMART?

- How can progress toward the objective be made measurable?

When objectives are not linked to clear business goals, unanticipated challenges often arise. This happens in areas that are seemingly unrelated to the objective in question. And in nine out of ten cases, it comes to light only later. As a result, the problems are less easily traced back to the objectives that were set incorrectly (too activity-oriented) at an earlier stage.

A second factor at play is the lack of understanding of the relationships, dependencies, and sequencing of other objectives. This contributes negatively to problem situations. The creation of a Goal/Objective Matrix helps to achieve the desired understanding and avoids the ambiguity outlined above.

Goal/Objective Matrix

In a Goal/Objective Matrix, the established goals are related to the intended objectives. Like all matrices, it shows the relationship between two elements. By creating this cross-mapping, it becomes clear which objectives contribute to the achievement of which goals.

Table 8-36. *Goal/Objective Matrix*

	Objectives				
	Objective A	Objective B	Objective C	Objective D	Objective E
Goals					
Goal A	X				
Goal B		X	X		
Goal C				X	
Goal D				X	X
Goal E		X			X

Organizations often struggle with how to determine whether they are successfully pursuing their strategy. Unfortunately, it is rarely possible to directly measure progress toward strategic goals and objectives. The widely used measure of customer satisfaction is a good example of this problem. There is no way to directly determine how satisfied a customer is. In fact, it is not clear that customers themselves always have a good understanding of this. Asking customers about their satisfaction seems to be the most direct way to get this measure, but customers who provide this information are not necessarily truthful (for a variety of reasons).

Objectives should therefore be specific, quantifiable, and achievable targets that need to be met in order to achieve the associated goals. Key performance indicators (KPIs) and related metrics provide the means to determine whether or not an objective has been met. See Section 8.5.1.2 for more details on making objective achievement measurable.

8.3.3.4. Initiatives

Table 8-37. *Deliverables of the focus area Initiatives*

Deliverable	Description
Objective/Initiative Matrix	Cross-mapping of objectives and initiatives

Initiatives are necessary to translate strategic goals into actionable projects and activities. Initiatives drive change and resource allocation, helping architects implement architectural changes that support the organization's strategic direction. Initiatives are used to effectively plan, manage, and execute the projects and activities that lead to the successful realization of the organization's strategy.

An initiative is a concept used to represent a planned action or project designed to achieve specific goals or objectives within the organization. Initiatives are concrete activities that are undertaken to implement changes, improve processes, or achieve desired outcomes as part of the overall strategy of the organization. They are directly linked to specific goals or objectives of the organization. Initiatives represent the actionable steps taken (projects, programs, or activities that implement architectural changes) to achieve these goals and ensure that the Enterprise Architecture is aligned with the strategic direction of the business. By defining specific initiatives, the Enterprise Architect can determine the necessary resources, such as funding, people, and technology, to execute the projects and achieve the desired results.

Initiatives play an important role in stakeholder management. They involve various stakeholders who are affected by or have an interest in the changes being implemented. Therefore, the architect must manage stakeholder expectations and communicate the impact of initiatives on their roles and responsibilities. A Communications Plan, as described in Chapter 8, Section 8.2.2.5, is used to accomplish this.

Initiatives also contribute to the strategic portfolio management capability, enabling the architect to prioritize and manage multiple initiatives based on their importance, alignment with strategic objectives, and available resources. Initiatives are used in roadmaps so that it is clear when the initiatives will be implemented (see Section 8.4.2). Plotting initiatives in a roadmap allows for the assignment of initiative owners (business actors or business roles).

Initiatives have defined objectives and outcomes, allowing architects to measure their success and effectiveness in achieving the desired results.

Now, the term initiative may be less familiar to the general public. Most people are probably more familiar with terms like project, program, or portfolio. From an Enterprise Architecture perspective, these are all types of initiatives [29].

Initiatives are sets or groupings of changes required to implement an intended change in the organization. Such an intended change usually stems from an organization's strategy. The required changes – that is, initiatives – are needed to achieve the desired outcome or end goal for the organization. To keep track of progress in implementing the strategy and achieving the desired results, the necessary initiatives are presented in a roadmap. A roadmap provides sufficient guidance for senior management to monitor the progress of planned changes. In addition to their valuable contribution to the roadmap, initiatives are often used as input for portfolio management [30].

Initiatives do not have a fixed scope in the sense that they exclusively represent a single project. Initiatives can encompass the scope of an entire portfolio as well as a single project or program. In agile terms, an initiative can also be a sprint.

Despite the fact that initiatives can come from anywhere (think existing lists, repositories, as well as people, including senior management, portfolio managers, project managers, etc.), in most cases they emerge from an organization's strategic agenda. The direction an organization sets based on its drivers and associated goals and objectives ultimately translates into a set or grouping of initiatives.

Within the architecture, initiatives are often linked to the objectives to which they contribute and the business unit or business role that sponsors them. A conceptual example of this is shown in Figure 8-19.

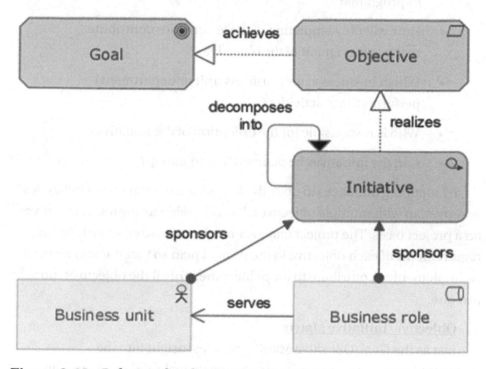

Figure 8-19. *Relationship between Initiatives, Business units/roles, and Objectives*

Like a business process, an initiative specifies the (high-level) activity or activities that must be performed to achieve an end result. Work packages (see Section 8.4.2) work in a similar way.

Each initiative should define the actions to be taken [30].

To develop a list of initiatives, senior management can be asked the following questions:

- What projects or programs are underway?
- What specific sets of activities are part of these projects or programs?
- How will the completion of these activities contribute to the achievement of the objectives?
- Which business actor (business unit or department) performs these activities?
- Who is responsible for the execution of the initiatives?
- Can the initiatives be planned in a roadmap?

By mapping initiatives to objectives, it becomes clear which initiatives may overlap with multiple objectives. It is advisable to approach initiatives on a project basis. The project manager can be instructed to include the requirements of each objective in the project plan so that the initiatives to be implemented contribute to the achievement of all the objectives, not just one.

Objective/Initiative Matrix

Just as the Goal/Objective Matrix provides insight into the relationships and interdependencies between goals and objectives, an Objective/Initiative Matrix provides a similar picture. In this case, it visualizes the relationship between objectives and initiatives.

Table 8-38. *Objective/Initiative Matrix*

	Initiatives				
	Initiative A	Initiative B	Initiative C	Initiative D	Initiative E
Objectives					
Objective A	X	X	X		
Objective B		X		X	X
Objective C			X		

Initiatives may overlap with multiple objectives. It is conceivable that the implementation of a particular initiative contributes (in part) to the achievement of one or more objectives. The degree of contribution may vary from objective to objective.

8.4. Execute

The third stage of the Enterprise Architecture Implementation Wheel is *Execute*. This stage consists of two steps, *Strategy* and *Roadmap*. The first step (Strategy) creates an overview that shows the translation of strategy to execution. This is often done in a spreadsheet format. The second step (Roadmap) handles the creation of two deliverables. The first deliverable is the realization of a Work Package Portfolio Map. This activity consists of identifying and shaping the initiatives to be implemented. The second deliverable is the creation of the Architecture Roadmap. The work packages are visually represented in the roadmap and plotted over time. This creates a high-level, multi-year schedule. Both steps are outlined in the following pages, along with a description for each of the key focus areas.

Table 8-39. *Third stage of the Enterprise Architecture Implementation Wheel*

Document	Define				Execute		Control
Information	Stakeholders	Maturity	Framework	Strategy	Strategy	Roadmap	Measure progress

8.4.1. Strategy

Table 8-40. *Deliverables of stage three – Execute/Strategy*

Deliverable	Description
Table from strategy to execution	Table of columns showing the translation of the organization's strategy to implementation

Once the drivers, goals, objectives, and initiatives have been established, determined, or distilled from the existing documents that describe the organization's direction, it is up to the Enterprise Architect to translate the strategy into a feasible implementation.

Ideally, a top-down approach should be used. This is why the TOGAF Standard states that business goals must be defined in the Preliminary Phase. In practice, this often works differently. Because an organization already exists, it usually has a description of its strategic direction. With existing organizations, there is no greenfield situation; an organization exists, runs, grows, and functions. It has to make do with what it has. As a result, a bottom-up approach must be used. This means using the strategic agenda that already exists, combined with the goals and objectives that have been set. Through reverse engineering, it is possible to look at what is already being done in the company and relate it to the existing strategic direction. In this way, there is a kind of retrospective accountability.

At a previous employer, I once sat down with senior management to distill themes from existing annual plans. These themes were later translated into goals.

The same exercise was done for each of the existing departments. This produced a considerable list of themes with the necessary overlap. Together with senior management, we went through the list of themes and were able to extract goals from them. The goals were then linked to the strategic direction of the organization.

A very different scenario occurred with another employer. Here, the hierarchical structure determined where you could – and, more importantly, could not – sit at the table. For this reason, I began to introduce a method for moving from strategy to execution.

The development of the methodology struck a chord with the board, and shortly thereafter I was asked to sit at the board table; there was interest in applying the methodology to the company's strategic agenda.

Whether a top-down or bottom-up approach is used, the method for translating strategy into execution remains the same. When a top-down approach is possible (in the case of a start-up, scale-up, or greenfield situation), the process associated with the method can be followed from beginning to end. A bottom-up approach requires an inventory of the organization across all architectural domains. This inventory can run in parallel with the implementation of the process described here. The inventory is used to map the organization. As the process in Figure 8-20 is executed, each step takes into account the existing situation. Each process step takes the current organization and projects the process steps onto the existing environment and setup.

The method cited here is a derivative of the approach that comes from the Business Architecture perspective. The approach is described in detail in the BIZBOK Guide [8], the *Business Architecture Body of Knowledge*, developed by the Business Architecture Guild.

The process of getting from the defined strategy to its implementation is carried out using five process steps.

Figure 8-20. Process model from strategy to implementation

The steps from the process model (Figure 8-20) are explained in more detail below.

Determine strategy: Strategy development consists of identifying drivers, goals, and intended (and measurable) objectives. The Enterprise Architecture plays an important role in understanding the impact of the chosen strategy on the organization. The content of this topic is discussed in Section 8.3.3. This section addresses (part of) the second stage of the Enterprise Architecture Implementation Wheel, *Define*.

Designate change: The process step of designing the required changes is characterized by identifying the changes needed to implement the strategy. This step requires intensive collaboration with senior management, other business leaders, strategists, and (IT) architects. Enterprise architecture is used in this step to further interpret and decompose the changes. It is also used to plan initiatives across the organization. Stage one of the Enterprise Architecture Implementation Wheel, *Document*, plays an important role here. Taking stock of the organization, which is necessary in a bottom-up approach to strategy implementation, is described in the first stage of the Implementation Wheel (see Section 8.2).

Determine roadmap: An architecture roadmap uses the captured initiatives. In this step, the Enterprise Architecture is used to shape the required initiatives, grouping and arranging them so that they can be used in a roadmap. Interdependencies between initiatives are also identified. Creating a roadmap with the required initiatives is discussed in Section 8.4, which deals with the third stage in the Enterprise Architecture Implementation Wheel, namely, *Execute*.

Develop solutions: The fourth step in the strategy to execution process is the development of solutions. Enterprise Architecture is not (directly) involved in designing solutions. That role is reserved for Solution Architecture. What is important in this step is to provide frameworks (see Section 8.3.2) and other forms of direction so that a solution can be arrived at.

Measure progress: Finally, measurable indicators are used to monitor the progress of strategy implementation. The fourth stage of the Enterprise Architecture Implementation Wheel, *Control* (see Section 8.5), explores this topic in more detail.

It is important to note in Figure 8-20 that the order of the steps shown is different from the order described in the Implementation Wheel. The first two steps from Figure 8-20 are shown in reverse order on the Implementation Wheel. This is where theory and practice diverge. Theory (e.g., the TOGAF Standard and the BIZBOK Guide) indicates that you should start by formulating goals and outcomes. This allows the strategy to move toward implementation. The theory is correct, but practice shows otherwise. In practice, translating the strategic agenda into concrete goals and objectives is not the first thing an Enterprise Architect will do. This was discussed in more detail when Chapter 8 was introduced.

Whether the goals already exist or are just being formulated, they can be combined with the defined objectives and initiatives (see Section 8.3.3) to form a table. An example is shown in Table 8-41. The method described here provides an overview. It also provides a view of the entire set of goals, objectives, and related initiatives. The dependencies of the organization's goals are visualized.

Table 8-41. *Example showing relations between drivers, goals, objectives, capabilites, and initiatives*

Drivers	Goals	Objectives	Capabilities	Initiatives
Driver A	Goal A.1	Objective A.1.1	Capability A	Initiative A.1.1.1
		Objective A.1.2		Initiative A.1.2.1
	Goal A.2	Objective A.2.1	Capability B	Initiative A.2.1.1
				Initiative A.2.1.2
	Goal A.3	Objective A.3.1	Capability A	Initiative A.3.1.1
		Objective A.3.2		Initiative A.3.2.1
Driver B	Goal B.1	Objective B.1.1	Capability A	Initiative B.1.1.1
	Goal B.2	Objective B.2.1	Capability D	Initiative B.2.1.1

To create a table such as Table 8-41, the following steps can be taken:

1. Start by recording the *strategic drivers* in the table. See Section 8.3.3.1 to define drivers.

2. Then complete the *goals* and associated *objectives*. Section 8.3.3.2 deals with goal formulation. Refer to Section 8.3.3.3 for the approach to arriving at objectives. Work with senior management and subject matter experts to formulate KPIs for the goals and identify corresponding metric thresholds. These metrics will be useful in stage four, *Control*. Section 8.3.3.2 explains how to use the SMART method to make goals and objectives measurable.

3. Determine what capabilities are needed to implement the initiatives. The identified capabilities can later be used to identify the *affected elements* from the various architectural domains. For example, consider business processes, business actors, information concepts, applications, and technology.

4. List the *initiatives* to achieve the objectives and those affected by each objective. Defining initiatives is discussed in Section 8.3.3.4.

Table 8-41 shows that a fictitious organization has two drivers (A and B). The first driver is assigned three goals (A.1, A.2, and A.3). Driver B is associated with two goals (B.1 and B.2).

Each goal is further subdivided into objectives. Goal A.1 has two objectives (A.1.1 and A.1.2). Goal A.2 has only one objective (A.2.1), and the third goal, like goal A.1, has two objectives (A.3.1 and A.3.2).

All goals and objectives are realized by the capabilities shown. In Table 8-41, it is easy to see that some capabilities are used multiple times to achieve different goals and objectives. The capabilities listed are things that the organization must be able to do or have (in terms of *abilities*). Capabilities contribute to the execution of *initiatives*.

Table 8-41 shows that there are several initiatives. The relationship of the initiatives to the previously named goals is represented by the sequence number. For example, Initiative A.1.1.1 has a relationship to Objective A.1.1 and indirectly to Goal A.1. Initiative B.2.1.1 has a relationship to Objective B.2.1, which in turn is the intended objective for achieving Goal B.2.

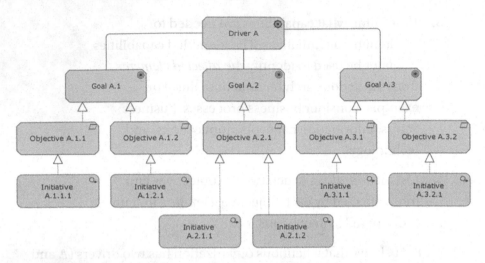

Figure 8-21. *Visualization of the data from Table 8-41*

At first glance, *visualizing* an existing organization's strategic agenda in this way may seem like a daunting task. In practice, it's not so bad. What makes it easier is having clear definitions and descriptions of all the elements mentioned (drivers, goals, and objectives). Without clear descriptions of these elements, creating and filling in a table like Table 8-41 becomes much more difficult.

Translating strategy into *execution* is, and will remain, one of the most difficult activities for an Enterprise Architect. Setting *concrete goals* (and corresponding objectives) is far from an easy task. These exercises require a great deal of time and effort from both the Enterprise Architect and senior management. It is not surprising that such an activity can easily take four to six months to complete.

Admittedly, using the suggested method and trying to complete the "from strategy to execution" table (Table 8-41) with sufficient calmness and attention is a rewarding activity.

I have used this method several times now, and the response from senior management is always that it gives so much insight into the relationship between the goals on the one hand and the initiatives to be taken on the other.

It ensures that the sense of being in control returns (or at least is reinforced) within the organization.

In Chapter 5, Section 5.3, the role of the Enterprise Architect was mentioned and the fact that this role is a key player in translating strategy into execution. Enterprise Architecture provides the necessary structure and framework for translating strategy into execution. There are several methods for managing this process. The method described in this book is based on Business Architecture as defined and articulated in the BIZBOK Guide [8].

Figure 8-22 visualizes the role that Enterprise Architecture plays in translating strategy into execution.

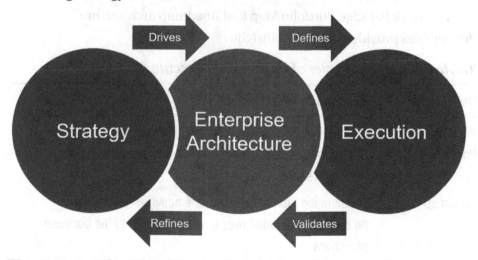

Figure 8-22. *The role of Enterprise Architecture in strategy execution*

Enterprise architecture is an essential and therefore indispensable part of strategy execution. Strategy is the catalyst for Enterprise Architecture. Architecture, in turn, defines the strategy and translates it into execution. Working backward, execution enables improvements to be made to the architecture. These improvements, in turn, ensure that the strategy is further refined by the architecture. The role of the Enterprise Architect is primarily to provide and apply the described methodology and to act as a guiding factor in translating the strategy into concrete goals, objectives, and initiatives. These strategic elements come together in a roadmap. This is where the initiatives are linked to the objectives and plotted over time. They can also be given a timetable.

8.4.2. Roadmap

In order to complete stage three of the Enterprise Architecture Implementation Wheel (Execute), and specifically the step of creating a roadmap, two things need to be accomplished. First, an overview of the initiatives to be planned that will flesh out the roadmap is needed. In addition, it is desirable to be able to relate these initiatives to business goals and objectives.

The Work Package Portfolio Map and Roadmap architecture deliverables provide the desired insight.

Table 8-42. *Deliverables of stage three – Execute/Roadmap*

Deliverable	Description
Work Package Portfolio Map	Overview of all activities (initiatives) required to implement the business strategy, plotted against business objectives and intended results
Roadmap	A schematic representation of the activities (initiatives) to be carried out, plotted over time and related to the business objectives

In Section 8.3.3.4, it was noted that high-level work packages are similar to initiatives. A cluster, set, or grouping of multiple work packages can be considered an initiative. These clusters of work packages often form a project, program, or even a portfolio. Initiatives do the same.

A work package generally does not describe an ongoing activity such as a business process. The subject of the work package is performed once and produces a well-defined end result. This is usually a goal or objective (see Figure 8-23). A work package can be used to model tasks within a project, entire projects, programs, or entire portfolios. In an agile context, a work package can be used to model the work done in an agile iteration (e.g., a sprint) or in a higher-level increment. Initiatives work similarly.

Work packages and initiatives are very alike. If there are any differences at all, they are so minimal that they are not worth mentioning. Over time, the distinction between work packages and initiatives will most likely blur to the point where only one architectural concept remains.

The TOGAF Standard defines a work package as a set of actions aimed at achieving one or more objectives.

A set of actions identified to achieve one or more objectives for the business. A work package can be a part of a project, a complete project, or a program [1].

ArchiMate, on the other hand, is more general in its definition and indicates that a work package achieves a result within certain time and resource constraints.

A work package represents a series of actions identified and designed to achieve specific results within specified time and resource constraints [12].

Conceptually, a work package is similar to a business process in that it consists of a series of related tasks aimed at producing a well-defined end result. In terms of content, a work package can be said to be a *unique and one-time process*; it performs a series of activities that lead to an end result. A work package can be described in much the same way as a process. Figure 8-23 illustrates the similarities (and differences) between a work package and a process.

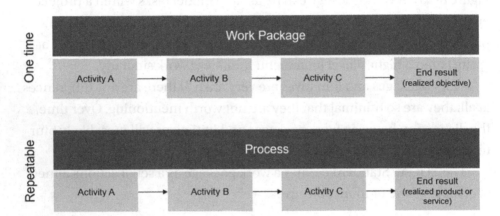

Figure 8-23. *Similarities and differences between work packages and processes*

Some time ago, I worked for a hospital. I worked with the board of directors to develop a roadmap based on the hospital's strategic agenda. One of the items on the roadmap was to implement new functionality in the Electronic Health Record (EHR).

This led to a project to implement a mobile application that would allow patients to schedule their appointments online.

At the time, the hospital did not have the necessary Digital patient management capability. However, this was one of the wishes expressed in an objective related to one of the hospital's goals, Digital hospital.

This goal included both structurally increasing efforts to further digitize patient data and providing digital services to patients.

The latter included the desire to allow patients to schedule appointments digitally. This required a new capability: Digital patient management.

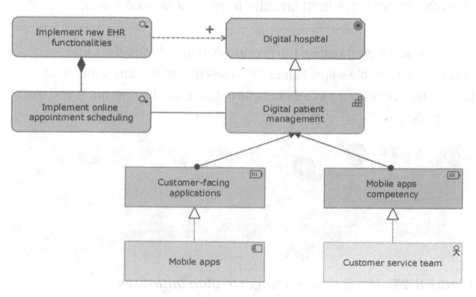

Figure 8-24. *Diagram showing the relationships between work package, goal, and capability*

Using the diagram in Figure 8-24, I was able to get the board to recognize that the Human Resources department should be instructed to hire qualified personnel to form a Customer service team.

This team was needed to provide appropriate support to patients using the new online appointment scheduling service.

Figure 8-24 shows the relationship between a work package and the
stated goal (Digital hospital) on the one hand, and a work package
and the capability to be created (Digital patient management) on the
other hand. The capability is supported by two resources. On the one
hand, the resource (Customer-facing applications) that is realized by
applications (Mobile apps), and on the other hand, the resource that
derives its existence from an actor (Customer service team).

Work packages translate the previously defined initiatives into
concrete, actionable steps. Figure 8-25 uses the implementation of an
Enterprise Architecture as an example to illustrate the operation and use of
work packages.

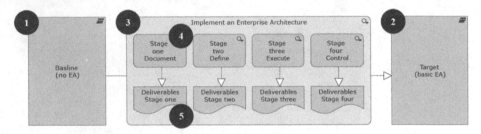

Figure 8-25. *Using work packages to plan initiatives*

Figure 8-25 shows an overview of (from left to right) the baseline
architecture, the set of work packages required to perform the activity, and
the end scenario, the target state.

The numbers in the colored circles have the following meanings:

1. **Baseline state:** The premise of this book is to
   arrive at the implementation of a basic Enterprise
   Architecture. The baseline state here means as
   much as the absence of an architecture. It still
   assumes that an Enterprise Architect is starting with
   an existing organization where architecture work is
   in its infancy. There is no Enterprise Architecture.

2. **Target state:** The desired target state: an implemented basic Enterprise Architecture.

3. **The parent work package:** This work package consists of several (smaller) work packages, namely, the stages from the Enterprise Architecture Implementation Wheel (see Figure 8-1).

4. **The Implementation Wheel stages:** These are shown here as separate work packages.

5. **The deliverables by stage:** These are the architecture deliverables for each stage from the Implementation Wheel. In Figure 8-25, the various deliverables from the four stages are grouped into one deliverable element for each stage.

A fully developed model of an Enterprise Architecture implementation, including the required deliverables and the objectives to be achieved, is shown in Appendix C: Example Work Package View.

Work Package Portfolio Map

An important architectural deliverable that serves as input to the Roadmap is the Work Package Portfolio Map. The goals and objectives contained in the Work Package Portfolio Map are elements that recur in the Roadmap. The initiatives defined in Section 8.3.3.4 can be converted to work packages (after all, initiatives and work packages are equivalent) and included as activities to be performed in the Roadmap. In this way, the initiatives/work packages are related to the previously defined goals and intended objectives.

A Work Package Portfolio Map consists of an overview of all work packages derived from the strategy. They are usually shown clustered or grouped together. A Work Package Portfolio Map is similar in structure and visualization to an Application Portfolio Catalog (Table 8-13).

Table 8-43. *Work Package Portfolio Map*

Work Package name	Work Package description	Associated with objective(s)	Associated with goal(s)
Work Package A	Stage one – Document	Objective A	Goal A
Work Package B	Stage two – Define	Objective B	
Work Package C	Stage three – Execute	Objective C	
Work Package D	Stage four – Control	Objective D	

A Work Package Portfolio Map forms the basis for the Roadmap.

Roadmap

A Roadmap is a timeline of previously defined initiatives in the form of work packages. It provides a visual overview of all the initiatives that need to be completed to achieve the organization's intended objectives (see Figure 8-26).

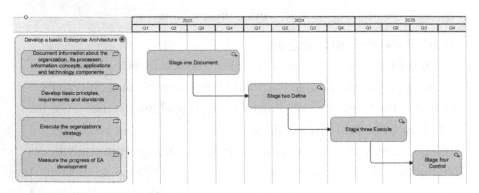

Figure 8-26. *Roadmap*

Using a good architecture tool (see Chapter 6, Section 6.4), it is easy to create a Roadmap. A Roadmap shows which work packages are related to which goals or intended objectives. Owners and (progress) states can be assigned to the work packages. Thus, a Roadmap can be used to monitor the progress of the implementation of the organization's strategy. It can also be used to visualize the cost of achieving the goals and objectives. By including the cost of executing the work packages as an attribute to the elements, a Roadmap can show how this relates to the realization of the intended results. Having an overview of the costs per work package can help prioritize projects or programs.

Using the previously created Work Package Portfolio Map (Section 8.4.2.), a first attempt at a Roadmap can be made. Place the goals or objectives on the left side of the Roadmap (vertical), and place the work packages from the Work Package Portfolio Map in the timeline area (horizontal).

This is where stages one, two, and three of the Enterprise Architecture Implementation Wheel come together. The Roadmap uses these stages to provide a clear and predictable view of the impact of the defined initiatives on the organization. The first two stages of the Enterprise Architecture Implementation Wheel produced deliverables. These deliverables help shape the necessary changes; they provide the information needed to make sense of the organizational changes. The deliverables are the end products of the individual work packages. Representing the work packages in the Roadmap clarifies when the architecture deliverables will be created and delivered.

A Roadmap is created by processing the work packages from the Work Package Portfolio Map and plotting them as activities over time. The Roadmap can be enriched by adding additional properties to the work packages. Examples include owners of the activities (business units or business roles), potential costs, and progress states (not started, pending, completed, canceled).

By adding additional properties to the work packages, it becomes possible to create cross sections and gain insight into who is responsible for what. This is helpful in monitoring the progress of the organization's goals and objectives. For example, color views can be used to visually illustrate the progress of projects. An example of a progress view is shown in Figure 8-27.

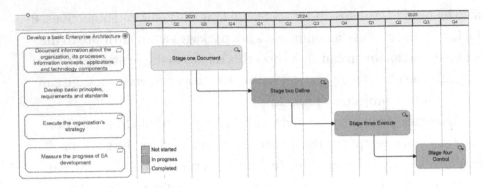

Figure 8-27. *Roadmap showing progress status*

Of course, the primary purpose of an architecture tool is to create architecture models and diagrams. An architecture tool is not a project management tool. It can create and display roadmaps to illustrate or justify project, program, or portfolio initiatives. However, it never replaces a project management plan or project progress reports.

8.5. Control

The fourth and final stage of the Implementation Wheel is *Control*. This stage consists of one step, *Measure progress*. The purpose of this step is to provide insight into the progress of the Enterprise Architecture implementation. The step is explained in the following pages, along with a description of its focus area.

Table 8-44. *Fourth stage of the Enterprise Architecture Implementation Wheel*

Document	Define				Execute			Control
Information	Stakeholders	Maturity	Framework	Strategy	Strategy	Roadmap		Measure progress

8.5.1. Measure Progress

In an organization where the Enterprise Architecture is mature, the focus is on making progress measurable in terms of achieving business goals and objectives. It is very different in an organization where the Enterprise Architecture is not (yet) mature. In an organization that has recently begun to work with architecture, progress in implementing the Enterprise Architecture is measured.

This involves measuring progress on two issues. One is the *creation of architecture deliverables*, and the other is the *achievement of the intended goal* of implementing an Enterprise Architecture.

8.5.1.1. Architecture Deliverables

It is important to determine what steps are required to achieve the creation of the desired architecture deliverables so that a percentage of progress can be assigned. A short step-by-step plan can be used to achieve the desired understanding of progress. This plan is shown in Figure 8-28 and should be applied to each individual topic for which progress is to be measured.

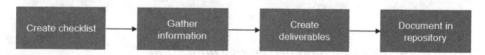

Figure 8-28. Steps to gather, process, and store information

Create checklist: First, create a checklist of activities that need to be planned and performed. Determine who needs to be approached to obtain the necessary information. Prepare questions and be sure to ask follow-up questions if some answers do not immediately lead to the desired information or level of detail. Try to keep the questions short and to the point, and limit them to a specific topic. Use the sample questions provided in the various sections of Chapter 8.

Gather information: To gather the necessary information, appointments need to be made with people in the organization. If the initial appointments do not lead directly to the desired information, be sure to schedule follow-up appointments or select other people from the organization.

Create deliverables: The information obtained can then be processed into catalogs, matrices, diagrams, and maps. This creates the architecture deliverables. The various deliverables are described in Sections 8.2 through 8.4.

Document in repository: Finally, it is important to capture the architecture deliverables in the architecture repository.

Once these four high-level steps have been successfully completed, that part is 100% realized. A fairly basic or more refined method can be used to determine what percentage of progress can be assigned to each step. The basic method assumes that a proportional percentage is assigned to all steps of the process to be performed. The more refined method involves assigning percentages based on, for example, the duration of each step.

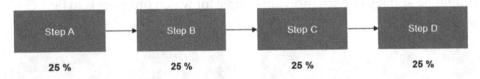

Figure 8-29. *Basic method percentage allocation*

In the basic method (Figure 8-29), a four-step method yields a rate of 25% for each step. When the more refined method (Figure 8-30) is used, for example, assigning a percentage based on the duration of each step, the distribution of percentages is often quite different. To illustrate, consider a process consisting of four steps, A, B, C, and D. Step A takes one hour to complete. Steps B and C each take two hours. Step D has a lead time of three hours. Using the more refined method of assigning percentages in proportion to the duration of the steps, the percentages for steps A through D would be 12½, 25, 25, and 37½%, respectively. Thus, assigning percentages based on the more refined method provides a more detailed picture of progress than using the basic concept of proportional percentages.

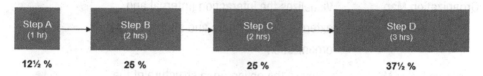

Figure 8-30. *Refined method percentage allocation*

When the two methods are applied to a process in which three of the four steps are completed, the basic method yields a rate of 75%. The more refined method shows that completion of the first three steps accounts for 62.5%. The latter method, therefore, provides a more realistic picture of the progress being made.

A common technique for charting the progress of individual deliverables is to use percentages and pie charts. Table 8-45 shows a fictitious example of progress by deliverable from the first stage of the Enterprise Architecture Implementation Wheel.

In Table 8-45, five values are used to express progress in percentages: 0, 25, 50, 75, and 100%. A small pie chart is included for each row in the table. The pie charts show the progress of *each individual item.*

Table 8-45. *Progress summary per deliverable of stage one –*
Document

Deliverable	Description	Progress
Organization Map	Visualizes the interaction (internal and external, with partners and suppliers) of the organization	
Business Roles Map	Displays the governance structure of the company	
Business Process Catalog	Listing of business processes in use, linked where possible to business functions and process owners	
Business Function/ Business Process Matrix	Cross-mapping of business functions and processes	
Organization/Business Process Matrix	Cross-mapping of business units and processes	
Information Map	Listing of information concepts in use	
Information Concept/ Business Process Matrix	Cross-mapping of information concepts and processes	
Application Portfolio Catalog	Listing of applications in use, both internal and external (e.g., cloud services purchased)	
Application/Information Concept Matrix	Cross-mapping of applications and information concepts	
Application/Business Process Matrix	Cross-mapping of applications and business processes	

(*continued*)

Table 8-45. (*continued*)

Deliverable	Description	Progress
Technology Portfolio Catalog	Enumeration of (server) systems in use, both internal and external (e.g. technological cloud services)	
Technology/Application Matrix	Cross-mapping of used (server) systems and applications	
Technology/Application Function Map	Mapping technology functionality onto application functionality	

A similar form can also be chosen to show progress *per stage*. The question with this form of abstraction is whether it provides a sufficiently meaningful view of progress. Since each stage is made up of several subcomponents, a summary of progress may not provide the most insight.

A third way to provide insight into progress is to use spider charts. This type of chart uses percentage values to plot the current state against the desired end state, 100%. Figure 8-31 shows the percentage progress of the steps from the Implementation Wheel associated with the first stage. The values from Table 8-45 are visualized in Figure 8-32.

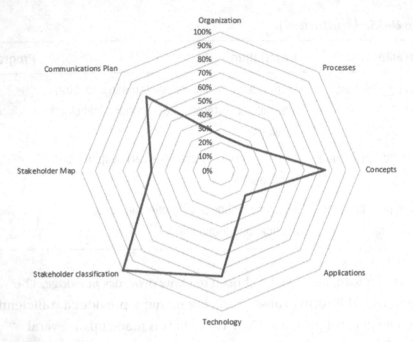

Figure 8-31. *Spider-chart progress chart per key focus area of stage one – Document*

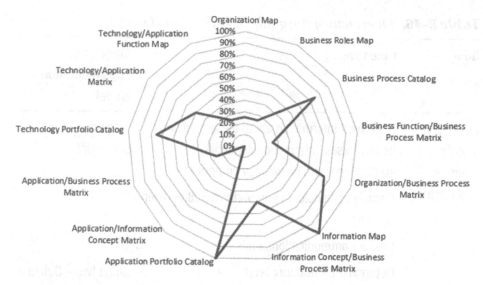

Figure 8-32. *Spider-chart progress chart per deliverable of stage one – Document*

Which form of visualization is chosen depends largely on personal preference. None of the forms described is more or less useful than the others.

8.5.1.2. Goals and Objectives

Section 8.3.3 provides guidance on how to set and formulate goals and objectives. An example of how to measure progress toward goals is given later in this chapter. The example assumes a stated goal, which is to successfully complete the implementation of a baseline Enterprise Architecture. The corresponding intended objectives and deliverables to be realized are shown in the steps of the Implementation Wheel.

Table 8-46 provides a schematic overview of the goal to be achieved and the intended deliverables.

Table 8-46. *Overview of the goal, objectives, and stages*

Goal	Objectives	Stage of the Implementation Wheel
Develop a basic Enterprise Architecture	Document information about the organization, its processes, information concepts, applications, and technology components	Stage one – Document
	Classify stakeholders and perform stakeholder analysis	
	Create Communications Plan	
	Determine EA maturity level	Stage two – Define
	Develop basic principles, requirements and standards	
	Define the organization's strategy	
	Execute the organization's strategy	Stage three – Execute
	Develop the roadmap	
	Measure the progress of EA development	Stage four – Control

To keep track of the objectives that need to be achieved, it is useful to create a summary table. Examples are shown in Table 8-46 and in Table 8-41 in Section 8.4.1. Using a summary table makes it clear which objectives are linked to which goals. You can also display specific initiatives in the table. In the example in Table 8-46, the individual initiatives are replaced by the stages (clustered initiatives) from the Enterprise Architecture Implementation Wheel.

For each initiative, it will be necessary to identify the activities that will ensure the successful completion of an initiative. In this way, a coherent overview is created of everything that is needed to – ultimately – realize the intended objectives and the associated goal.

One tool for monitoring the *sequence* of implementation of initiatives and activities is the use of a Roadmap (see Section 8.4.2). In a roadmap, the interdependencies between initiatives can be visualized (see also Figure 8-26). The project or program management capability can provide the necessary guidance.

Progress management is also important. Section 8.5.1.1 showed how to determine the *progress* of activities and initiatives. The insight gained at a detailed level can then be translated into progress against business objectives. Progress against business objectives should be discussed at management level, preferably on a regular basis. The frequency and form of information to the appropriate stakeholders is determined and recorded in the Communications Plan (see Table 8-23 in Section 8.2.2.5).

8.5.1.3. Dashboards

In Section 8.5.1.1, spider charts (Figure 8-31 and Figure 8-32) were used to visualize the progress of specific deliverables and stages from the Implementation Wheel. In addition to using this type of chart, it is also possible to display progress on specific topics in a dashboard (Figure 8-33).

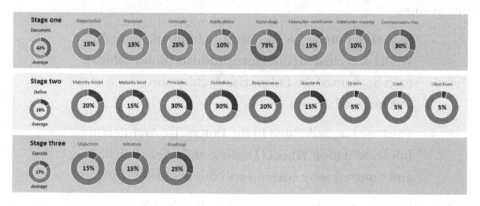

Figure 8-33. *Example of a dashboard*

Dashboards are an excellent tool for displaying the overall progress of a particular topic. Especially at the management level, dashboards like the one shown in Figure 8-33 are in demand. A dashboard omits most substantive information and simply shows the progress of an issue or program using easy-to-read and interpret graphs (such as pie charts) or gauges.

A graph can be created based on percentages that indicate how much of a particular topic has been accomplished (e.g., using donut charts, as shown in Figure 8-33). When progress data is included in a dashboard, it provides a good visual overview: a kind of one-page progress view. It is important to note that a dashboard is only as good and useful as the accuracy with which the progress of the topics it displays is determined. A dashboard is nothing more than a way to visualize what has been measured through a thorough process (as described in Section 8.5.1.1).

8.6. Summary

Chapter 8 described the actual implementation of a basic Enterprise Architecture.

- Using the Enterprise Architecture Implementation Wheel and clear architecture products (deliverables), each domain of the Enterprise Architecture was mapped.

- The four stages defined in the Enterprise Architecture Implementation Wheel (*Document, Define, Execute,* and *Control*) were covered and discussed step by step.

- Personal experiences, examples, and detailed explanations were used to work toward implementing a basic Enterprise Architecture.

CHAPTER 9

Next Steps

Chapter 9 discusses the steps that can be taken after the basic Enterprise Architecture has been implemented. In doing so, it looks beyond the horizon of the initial implementation and provides guidance for further expansion and growth in the maturity of the Enterprise Architecture. For each stage of the Enterprise Architecture Implementation Wheel, it identifies the growth opportunities that exist and the architecture products that can play a role in further maturing the Enterprise Architecture.

9.1. The Next Level

Now that the dust has settled on the initial implementation of a basic Enterprise Architecture, it is time to look cautiously ahead. The gaze can be turned forward to determine what can be done to take the architecture effort to the next level. One of the tools that can be used is the Maturity model (see Section 8.3.1.1) described in the *Define* stage (stage two) of the Enterprise Architecture Implementation Wheel. For each topic in the model, one can look carefully at the next level. From this, it is possible to derive what initiatives are needed to further increase the maturity of working with architecture. All steps and activities to be taken must remain consistent with the strategic direction of the organization. When change occurs, the Enterprise Architecture should reflect that change.

© Eric Jager 2023
E. Jager, *Getting Started with Enterprise Architecture*,
https://doi.org/10.1007/978-1-4842-9858-9_9

Processing or incorporating the changes begins by going through the stages of the Enterprise Architecture Implementation Wheel again. Like the ADM of the TOGAF Standard, the Implementation Wheel follows its iterative nature.

In addition to changes in direction, it is also possible to bring the Enterprise Architecture itself to a more mature state. As stated at the beginning of this book, there is much more that can be accomplished in the area of Enterprise Architecture. This book has only described the basics.

The *Document* stage of the Implementation Wheel (stage one) described the creation of a number of architecture deliverables. There are more than were described in that stage. Some of the undescribed deliverables are useful in certain situations and should be delivered as the next step. The TOGAF Standard provides a comprehensive overview of all useful deliverables to be produced [22].

The *Document* stage continues to play an important role in the evolution of the Enterprise Architecture. Each time a project or program is initiated, this stage can be used to map the information needed for that initiative. The use of catalogs, matrices, diagrams, and maps also plays an important role in this process.

The *Define* stage (stage two) determined the current and desired maturity of the architecture capability. With every iteration of the Implementation Wheel, the level of architectural maturity within the organization will be addressed. Architects can derive what initiatives are needed to further increase the maturity of working with architecture.

The *Define* stage also focused on defining basic principles, requirements, and standards. Especially in the area of requirements and standards, there is still much to be gained. For example, an attempt can be made to create standard sets of requirements that can be used in different standard situations. An example of this is the creation of a set of requirements for the purchase or provision of cloud services. The same requirements can be used over and over again for this category of services. By capturing them and making them available in a set, the process of gathering requirements is accelerated, and the purchase or deployment of a cloud service can occur sooner. A set of requirements can also be used when hiring staff. Requirements for specific functions are relatively easy to capture in a set of requirements.

The *Execute* stage (stage three) provides opportunities to increase the use of architecture roadmaps. Roadmaps can be used for a variety of initiatives and are not limited to use during the implementation of an Enterprise Architecture. Roadmaps are valuable deliverables that can add value especially during the implementation of projects or programs. Mapping and visualizing the interdependencies between initiatives provides very useful information and insights.

Finally, the *Control* stage (stage four) allows the Enterprise Architect to use charts and dashboards to keep track of the progress and realization of various initiatives, goals, and objectives. The way in which progress data is displayed and visualized can be refined and complemented. The level of detail in the charts can also be tailored to the needs of the organization. The same goes for what is or is not displayed on a dashboard.

In fact, the evolution of Enterprise Architecture never stops. The organization is always moving, and the Enterprise Architecture Implementation Wheel keeps on turning, so to speak. And while the organization may be temporarily in calmer waters, the market is in full swing. The Enterprise Architecture must move with the internal and external waves. It must be able to grow in scope and maturity. This is the constant challenge for the Enterprise Architect.

9.2. Summary

Chapter 9 discussed the steps that can be taken after the basic Enterprise Architecture has been implemented.

- It looked beyond the horizon of the initial implementation and provided guidance for further expansion and growth in the maturity of the Enterprise Architecture.

- For each stage of the Enterprise Architecture Implementation Wheel, it identified the growth opportunities that exist and the architecture products that can play a role in further maturing the Enterprise Architecture.

CHAPTER 10

Architecture Application

This chapter uses a very concrete example to show how an implemented basic Enterprise Architecture can be used to address a strategic issue. The example uses a fictitious organization facing a challenge. The application of the various Enterprise Architecture products illustrates and emphasizes the structure that a baseline implementation can provide in moving from strategy to execution.

10.1. Lemon-A-de

Now that all the stages of the Enterprise Architecture Implementation Wheel have been completed, a foundation has been laid upon which Enterprise Architecture issues can be executed. The creation of the various architecture deliverables has provided insight into the organizational structure, processes and information concepts, applications, and technology components in use. There is also an understanding of the strategic direction of the enterprise, and specific goals and measurable objectives are defined. Finally, there is a picture of how the progress of the implementation of the strategy can be visualized.

© Eric Jager 2023
E. Jager, *Getting Started with Enterprise Architecture*,
https://doi.org/10.1007/978-1-4842-9858-9_10

Using a fictional scenario, this basic Enterprise Architecture can be used to achieve the goals of a non-existent company. The company Lemon-A-de is, of course, not comparable to an existing organization; the setup of Lemon-A-de is greatly simplified in this example. The fictitious company is used for illustration purposes only.

The organization Lemon-A-de exists for about two years. As the name suggests, the company focuses on selling A-quality lemonade. The first year and a half of its existence was spent on writing a long-term strategy rather than on producing and selling lemonade. In the last 18 months, 22,500 bottles of lemonade have been produced. 1,000 bottles of lemonade were sold per month. Little profit has been made, just under 10%. The organization is relatively small, with six employees. Figure 10-1 shows the layout of the organization using a Business Roles Map.

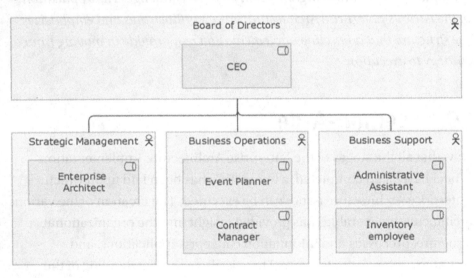

Figure 10-1. *Business Roles Map*

Over the past few months, Lemon-A-de has signed contracts with suppliers of limes, recyclable lemonade bottles, label makers, promotional material printers, and large event organizers. Lemon-A-de's relationships are shown in an Organization Map (Figure 10-2).

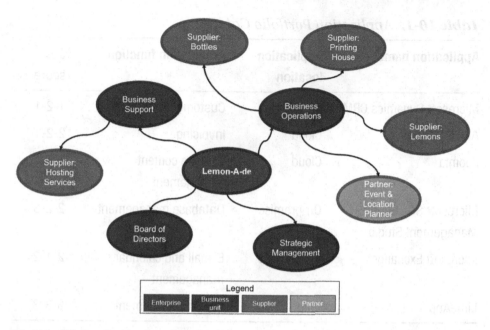

Figure 10-2. Organization Map

The company uses six applications to manage its internal operations. These include a customer management system, an invoicing tool, a website and associated content management system (CMS), a database application to store customer and website data, and a calendar management system to keep track of events Lemon-A-de attends. A custom application is also used to record the flavors of the lemonade to be produced. This LimeApp is also available as an app for mobile devices. The billing tool, website, CMS, and app are outsourced to a third party that provides web hosting and app development. The application landscape is shown in Table 10-1.

Table 10-1. *Application Portfolio Catalog*

Application name	Application location	Application function	CIA score
Microsoft Dynamics CRM	On-premise	Customer management	1-2-1
AFAS	Cloud	Invoicing	2-2-1
Joomla	Cloud	Website content management	1-1-1
Microsoft SQL Server Management Studio	On-premise	Database management	2-2-3
Microsoft Exchange	On-premise	E-mail and calendar management	2-1-2
LimeApp	Cloud	Flavor management	3-3-3

Lemon-A-de makes lemonade. Getting the right flavor and creating new flavors is meticulously tracked in the LimeApp. No matter where employees are located, they are always in touch with LimeApp. This ensures the company's ability to add new flavors to the app or tweak existing flavors based on customer feedback. Lemon-A-de employees receive this feedback when they attend events.

An inventory of all technology components owned by Lemon-A-de and purchased from external parties was created. The components were recorded in a Technology Portfolio Catalog (Table 10-2).

Table 10-2. *Technology Portfolio Catalog*

Technology component	Operating system	OS version number	Technology location	Purpose
Server A	Microsoft Windows Server	2019	On-premise	CRM application server
Server B	Microsoft Windows Server	2019	On-premise	CRM database server
Server C	Microsoft Windows Server	2022	On-premise	File server
Server D	Red Hat Server	8.5	Cloud	Application server
Server E	Red Hat Server	8.5	Cloud	Web server
Server F	Microsoft Windows Server	2022	On-premise	Database server
Server G	Microsoft Windows Server	2022	On-premise	E-mail server
Server H	Red Hat Server	8.5	Cloud	Web application server

A cross-mapping of technology components and applications was also performed. This cross-mapping is shown in Table 10-3.

Table 10-3. *Technology/Application Matrix*

| | Application component | | | | | |
	Microsoft Dynamics CRM	AFAS	Joomla	Microsoft SQL Server Management Studio	Microsoft Exchange	LimeApp
Technology component						
Server A	X					
Server B	X					
Server C						
Server D		X				
Server E			X			
Server F				X		
Server G					X	
Server H						X

Lemon-A-de has developed an ambitious strategy for the next two years. Two drivers play an important role: market share and revenue. The CEO believes it is important to participate in events that will increase Lemon-A-de's brand awareness. In her opinion, this will also increase sales of the lemonade produced. However, this will depend on Lemon-A-de being able to produce enough to meet the expected increase in demand. Efficient use of human resources can contribute to this, as can reviewing agreements with suppliers.

To implement the strategy, Lemon-A-de defined goals and objectives and asked the Enterprise Architect to determine the impact of the strategy on operations. Any changes to the organizational structure, process flows, application landscape, or even technology can be implemented with impunity. Achieving the set goals is paramount. Money is not a factor. Lemon-A-de's strategy is represented by a Goal/Objective Diagram (Figure 10-3).

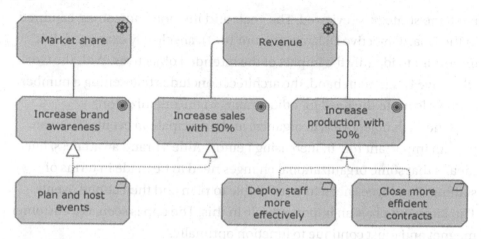

Figure 10-3. *Goal/Objective Diagram*

The established strategy feels like an ambitious plan, agrees the CEO. Ambitious, but achievable. The Enterprise Architect is asked to visualize the implementation of the strategy in a roadmap. At the same time, the architect should indicate if and where there are bottlenecks. If so, the CEO would like to see a plan of action with a proposed solution. Finally, the CEO indicated that she wanted to be well informed, but that it was also important to involve the rest of the organization in the implementation of the strategy.

10.2. Developing Lemon-A-de's Architecture

First, the strategy is reviewed. The goals and intended outcomes, captured in the Goal/Objective Diagram (Figure 10-3), are closely examined. It is important to identify the impact of the intended objectives. With the Goal/Objective Diagram in hand, the architect concludes that setting a number of goals leads to the need for adjustments in the organization.

One such objective is to organize and participate in events. This can play an important role in increasing Lemon-A-de's brand awareness, but means that some organizational changes need to be made in terms of staffing. Employees need to be available to plan and then attend events. The LimeApp plays an important role in this. The app is seen as a customer magnet and must continue to function optimally.

Looking at the Business Roles Map (Figure 10-1), it quickly becomes apparent that there are no roles defined for employees who regularly attend events. The company has an Event Planner, but no one who actually attends events and promotes Lemon-A-de. Since one of the goals is to increase revenue, roles need to be defined for people to attend events. This will require an increase in staff.

To increase brand awareness, the brand needs to be promoted at events. This will require staff to attend events. A campaign has been designed to give potential customers access to a restricted area of the LimeApp where they can make suggestions for new flavors of lemonade. This initiative should increase sales of the lemonade and raise brand awareness. As a result, production should be increased. This, too, will require additional staff.

Currently, one employee is dedicated to planning events. If the goal of increasing brand awareness is to be achieved, several events will need to be organized. However, planning such an event takes a lot of time, and the staff member indicates that he is not in a position to plan additional events. Again, an increase in capacity seems necessary. Perhaps, this could be combined with the newly hired staff attending the events. Hiring three additional people will make it possible to organize one event per quarter, but attendance is not yet an issue. This would mean hiring four additional people to actually attend the scheduled events. Another option would be to hire two of the four Event Planners as Event Hosts. While this cuts the number of scheduled events in half, it also reduces the need for hiring. On the other hand, it increases brand awareness by 50%.

The Enterprise Architect creates a diagram (Figure 10-4) that illustrates both options. The diagram shows that there is a need to have the ability to organize events. This need is specifically expressed in the role of the Event Planner. In order to properly fulfill the *Brand Management* capability, it is necessary to hire additional staff. Hiring staff ensures that events can be planned and executed. The way in which events are planned and executed depends on the decision made regarding the hiring of staff. If fewer people are hired, the existing staff will need to be trained. This addresses the *Competency Management* capability. If the decision is made to hire the proposed seven people, then there is no need for training.

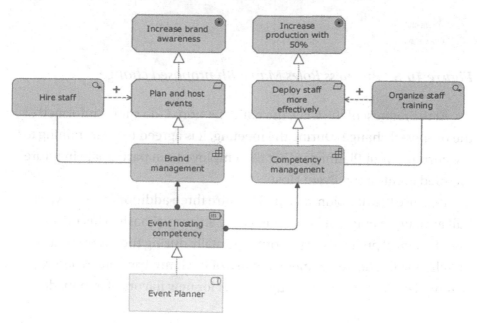

Figure 10-4. *Diagram showing the two options*

The two options are presented to the CEO during one of the recurring meetings. The CEO decides to hire fewer people. This means hiring three Event Planners, one of whom will plan events with the Event Planner already on staff. The other two Event Planners are hired as Event Hosts. The Business Roles Map is updated to reflect this decision (see Figure 10-5).

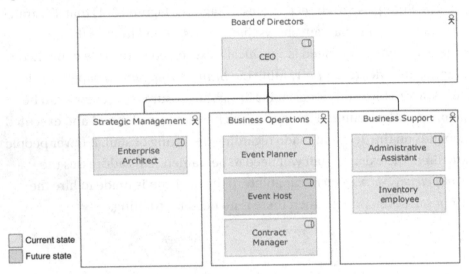

Figure 10-5. *Business Roles Map with proposed change*

At the request of the CEO, the entire Lemon-A-de staff is informed of the proposed change. During the meeting, it is agreed to offer training to the current Event Planner so that this employee can participate in future planned events as an Event Host.

Because the decision was made to hire three additional employees, half as many events can be scheduled on an annual basis. This means that the LimeApp needs to perform optimally during the events that can be scheduled. The deployment and use of the LimeApp, which allows potential customers to make suggestions for new flavors of lemonade, becomes much more important because of this decision. There are now two times a year when the app can be deployed instead of the planned *four*.

The Enterprise Architect examines the technology behind the app and concludes that the technology components still comply with the organization's lifecycle management policy. This is done using the Technology Portfolio Catalog (Table 10-2) and the Technology/Application Matrix (Table 10-3). Component replacement is not currently an issue. However, the architect instructs the application management team to keep a close eye on the number of connections to and from the app. A report on LimeApp's performance should be delivered twice a year.

A second issue that caught the Enterprise Architect's attention was increasing production. It quickly becomes clear that Lemon-A-de needs to work smarter and more efficiently if it is to achieve its goal of *increasing production by 50%*. Wherever possible, personnel must be used more effectively. The architect decides to take a close look at the process design. There may be things that can be improved.

In creating the Application/Business Process Map (Table 10-4), it becomes clear that some processes cannot be linked to applications. This means that these processes are most likely not automated. Further investigation reveals that manual actions are indeed taking place. These actions are mainly in the area of *bottle artwork handling*. This process is currently performed by the Inventory employee.

Table 10-4. Application/Business Process Map

Application component	Business process							
	Handle customer information	Handle payment	Publish content	Store data	Handle bottle artwork	Send message	Schedule event	Manage flavors
Microsoft Dynamics CRM	X							
AFAS		X						
Joomla			X					
Microsoft SQL Server Management Studio				X				
Microsoft Exchange						X	X	
LimeApp								X

The architect also includes in the strategy implementation proposal the need to adjust contracts with bottle suppliers. The Organization Map (Figure 10-2) is used to identify the suppliers that provide the labels and bottles. The architect's suggestion is to ask the suppliers to provide the bottles with the necessary artwork. This way, the bottles are delivered ready to use, and no manual (and time-consuming) action is required by the Inventory employee. The time saved can be used to fill the bottles with lemonade. This benefits production.

The Enterprise Architect looked at all facets of translating strategy into execution. Specific work packages are created that contain the various initiatives to be implemented. The architect relates the work packages to the existing strategy and visualizes them using a Goal/Initiative Diagram (Figure 10-6). The initiatives are incorporated into a roadmap and plotted over time.

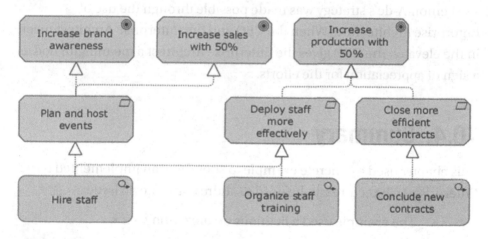

Figure 10-6. *Goal/Initiative Diagram*

The Enterprise Architect also creates a Communications Plan. This plan is used on a regular basis to ensure that stakeholders are properly informed. In accordance with the CEO's wishes, all company employees are kept well informed about the progress of changes within the organization.

10.3. A Few Years Later

Lemon-A-de is a successful company that is a national leader in the sale of A-quality lemonade. They are known for the quality of the lemonade and the wide variety of flavors. What sets them apart from the competition is the opportunity they give customers to come up with their own ideas for new flavors. This is something that customers take advantage of on a regular basis. Lemon-A-de's product line continues to grow, as does its market share.

During a recent meeting, the Enterprise Architect indicated that the LimeApp was still performing adequately in terms of current usage. However, when defining the strategy for the next few years, it is important to take into account a possible expansion of capacity, as the app will not be able to handle the same growth as in the past years.

Lemon-A-de's strategy was made possible through the use of Enterprise Architecture. When the CEO and the Enterprise Architect meet in the elevator, the CEO gives the Enterprise Architect a meaningful nod as a sign of appreciation for the efforts.

10.4. Summary

This chapter used a concrete example to show how an implemented basic Enterprise Architecture can be used to address a strategic issue.

- The example used a fictitious organization facing a challenge.

- The application of the various Enterprise Architecture products illustrated and emphasized the structure that a baseline implementation can provide in moving from strategy to execution.

CHAPTER 11

Closing Remarks

The purpose of this book is to provide insight into how a basic Enterprise Architecture can be established within an existing organization. I have tried to illustrate, substantiate, and entertain with the experiences I have had over the years with a variety of employers. Based on these experiences, I have developed my own view of how a basic Enterprise Architecture can be established within an existing organization.

Architecture frameworks are a more than valuable tool in the voyage of discovery that is the implementation of an Enterprise Architecture. Although frameworks are theoretically correct in their construction and proposed sequential approach, practice proves to be more recalcitrant.

Implementing Enterprise Architecture involves not only mapping the organization, processes, information concepts, application landscape, and technology in use, but also communicating architectural thinking. Many organizations are initially critical of this concept. Only when it becomes clear that working with architecture is different from changing the way they work, do most organizations change their minds. Working with architecture is *complementary* to what the organization is already doing.

Using the challenges faced by the fictional company Lemon-A-de, I have tried to show how a basic Enterprise Architecture can be used to help an organization implement its intended strategy. Although Lemon-A-de is a relatively small organization, the power of applying Enterprise Architecture in translating strategy into execution becomes clear.

© Eric Jager 2023
E. Jager, *Getting Started with Enterprise Architecture*,
https://doi.org/10.1007/978-1-4842-9858-9_11

Implementing Enterprise Architecture, like getting an organization to work with architecture, takes a long time. As simple as it sounds, the perseverer wins. The organization will slowly begin to see the benefits of working with architecture, and the Enterprise Architect will increasingly become a regular guest at the boardroom table. The setting of frameworks and the application of the strategic direction of the organization to achieve goals and objectives will eventually give the organization a foothold. These issues will increasingly appear on various agendas within the organization. In this way, people will become more familiar with working with architecture.

The structure that Enterprise Architecture provides, the feeling of being in control of the management of the organization, the feeling of being in control of the initiatives that are underway, are all examples of the experience that an organization gets when it moves to working with architecture. And when the people within the organization take it upon themselves to embed this way of working in their own activities and initiatives, it can definitely be called a moment of victory.

Implementing Enterprise Architecture is a journey in itself. And it can be an unforgettable journey. Like all things in life, it starts at the beginning: *Getting Started with Enterprise Architecture.*

APPENDIX A

Example Information Map

Example Information Map

Information Concept	Information Concept Category	Information Concept Definition	Information Concept Type	Related Information Concept
Accreditation	Primary	A certification, such as of origin to verify provenance of food item, manufactured part, or other material, or of competence in a specified subject or area of expertise – awarded by a duly recognized and respected third party – as it applies to a public sector entity or constituent	Internal, external	Energy, license, legislation, policy, partner, constituent

(continued)

E. Jager, *Getting Started with Enterprise Architecture*,
https://doi.org/10.1007/978-1-4842-9858-9_12

		Example Information Map		
Information Concept	**Information Concept Category**	**Information Concept Definition**	**Information Concept Type**	**Related Information Concept**
Agreement	Primary	A set of legally binding rights and obligations between two or more legal entities	Bilateral, unilateral, express, implied, executed, executory, aleatory	Asset, claim, channel, content, constituent, conveyor, financial account, government service, investment, network, operation, order, partner, policy, payment, tax

(*continued*)

| | | Example Information Map | | |
Information Concept	Information Concept Category	Information Concept Definition	Information Concept Type	Related Information Concept
Human resource	Primary	Individuals who have, plan to have, or have had a legal agreement with the organization, or otherwise provide work for hire, which may or may not include compensation and other benefits on a temporary or permanent basis	Contractor, employee, volunteer	Accreditation, case, competency, constituent, meeting, incident, inquiry, job, license, location, message, partner, payment, plan, policy, initiative, research, work item, vote

(continued)

Example Information Map				
Information Concept	Information Concept Category	Information Concept Definition	Information Concept Type	Related Information Concept
License	Primary	An authorization to perform a regulated activity, awarded by duly recognized governmental agency or third party, applied to an individual or organization, to engage in an activity, such as fishing, or use of regulated objects, such as modes transportation or hazardous materials	Commercial, conveyor, animal, builder, sport	Accreditation, competency, government service, market, location, job, plan, policy, initiative, strategy, training course, constituent, channel

(continued)

Example Information Map				
Information Concept	Information Concept Category	Information Concept Definition	Information Concept Type	Related Information Concept
Message	Primary	A verbal, written, recorded, or digitally represented communication, including missives, notifications, alerts, and other internally or externally targeted communication about the organization's mission, products, plans, activities, and other focal points	Internal (inbound), external (outbound)	Asset, brand, meeting, event, human resource, inquiry, legislation, policy, initiative, strategy, work, agreement, constituent, channel, partner, government service, financial account, financial transaction

The example provided in this appendix can be downloaded from *https://eawheel.com/book/media*.

APPENDIX B

Example Maturity Model

	Ad hoc (level 1)	Repeatable (level 2)	Defined (level 3)	Managed (level 4)	Optimal (level 5)
Strategy and vision	Architecture activities are not formally initiated and happen ad hoc	The need to define processes and standards is recognized An architect is present within the organization Architecture compliance is not defined	Architecture processes are ad hoc and inconsistent Projects are implemented without architecture contribution Compliance with architecture is informal and unstructured and cannot be measured	The documentation of business drivers, goals and objectives, architecture standards, etc. are not formally defined	The organization recognizes that staff need to become more familiar with working with architecture Some departments or employees do not support the architecture effort

(continued)

© Eric Jager 2023
E. Jager, *Getting Started with Enterprise Architecture*,
https://doi.org/10.1007/978-1-4842-9858-9_13

	Ad hoc (level 1)	Repeatable (level 2)	Defined (level 3)	Managed (level 4)	Optimal (level 5)
Architecture governance	The organization has started drafting a vision for EA EA tasks, activities, and required resources are identified The organization has determined the architecture methodology to be used	The need for governance has been identified Clear roles and responsibilities are established Senior management is aware of the need for EA EA awareness activities begin to emerge or are being developed	The architecture method is beginning to be reused to capture crucial EA information The need for integration between project management and EA has been identified Development of a compliance process has started so that projects and improvements are in line with EA standards	Drivers, goals, and objectives have been identified EA framework has been established There is a need for an EA repository to capture architecture products	The organization has started raising awareness and understanding of EA concepts and processes EA concepts are introduced and occasionally used and discussed in meetings

(*continued*)

	Ad hoc (level 1)	Repeatable (level 2)	Defined (level 3)	Managed (level 4)	Optimal (level 5)
Architecture method and process	EA deployment is clearly defined, including governance roles and responsibilities There is a roadmap for further EA development EA activities are implemented according to the established plan	Architecture governance is defined (a consultative body has been created) There are clear roles and responsibilities Senior management receives training on architecture and its benefits	Templates are used so that capture of information is consistent EA is integrated into strategic planning A formal EA compliance process is defined and is an integral part of EA The EA compliance process is consistently followed throughout the company	Classification of existing standards is consistent Documentation of drivers, goals, and objectives is consistent EA frameworks are formally accepted in the organization	The organization starts to operate as a team, using the defined architecture and standards Senior management participates in various EA consultation forums where the business is also represented

(continued)

	Ad hoc (level 1)	Repeatable (level 2)	Defined (level 3)	Managed (level 4)	Optimal (level 5)
Architecture deliverables	The EA is evaluated, and adjustments are identified to improve the EA The organization records metrics to measure progress in developing the EA	The communication process is revised to improve EA activity EA awareness training is included in the onboarding of new employees Statistics are recorded to measure the effectiveness of the EA communication process	EA is used to guide organizational development Compliance with EA standards has become commonplace across the enterprise The organization records metrics to measure the effectiveness of EA processes and templates	Documentation of drivers, goals, and objectives has become a standard activity Documentation and classification of products, services, and standards have become regular activities EA frameworks are actively used in projects	Staff throughout the organization have a good understanding of the architecture principles The organization records metrics to measure awareness, participation, acceptance, and satisfaction against the EA

(*continued*)

	Ad hoc (level 1)	Repeatable (level 2)	Defined (level 3)	Managed (level 4)	Optimal (level 5)
Business alignment	Action plans are proactively implemented to increase EA effectiveness based on measured data	The organization collaborates with similar organizations exchanging ideas to improve their EA Measurement data is used to communicate and deploy the EA even better	Business influences technology and technology influences business Captured metrics are used to proactively identify and make improvements to EA processes, the EA framework, and/ or architecture products	Captured business and technology information is used to proactively identify technology that will improve business operations	Departments work together as contributors to the architecture and its processes

The example provided in this appendix can be downloaded from *https://eawheel.com/book/media.*

APPENDIX C

Example Work Package View

© Eric Jager 2023
E. Jager, *Getting Started with Enterprise Architecture*,
https://doi.org/10.1007/978-1-4842-9858-9_14

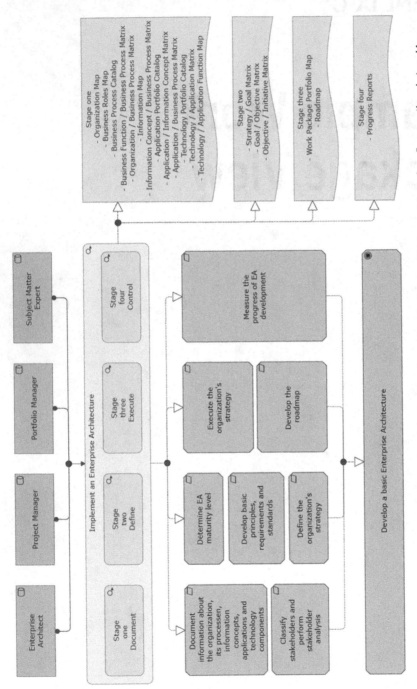

The example provided in this appendix can be downloaded from *https://eawheel.com/book/media.*

References

[1]   The Open Group. *The TOGAF® Standard,*
       10th Edition, Introduction and Core Concepts.
       's-Hertogenbosch: Van Haren Publishing, 2022.

[2]   Zachman, John. "The Zachman Framework," *A*
       Framework for Information Systems Architecture.
       1987 [Online]. Available: www.zachman.com/images/
       ZI_PIcs/ibmsj2603e.pdf.

[3]   Zachman, John. "Evolution of the Zachman
       Framework," www.zachman.com/resource/
       ea-articles/54-the-zachman-framework-
       evolution-by-john-p-zachman, 2009.

[4]   Ylimaki, Tanja, and Halttunen, Veikko. "Method
       Engineering in Practice: A Case of Applying the
       Zachman Framework in the Context of Small
       Enterprise Architecture Oriented Projects,"
       Information, Knowledge, Systems Management,
       vol. 5, no. 3, pp. 189–209, 2006.

[5]   Jager, Eric. "The many definitions of Enterprise
       Architecture," https://eawheel.com/blog/
       2023/04/the-many-definitions-of-enterprise-
       architecture/, 2023.

© Eric Jager 2023
E. Jager, *Getting Started with Enterprise Architecture,*
https://doi.org/10.1007/978-1-4842-9858-9

[6]   ISO (International Organization for
      Standardization), "Systems and software
      engineering – Architecture description,"
      www.iso.org/standard/50508.html, 2011.

[7]   The Open Group. "Architecture in the Context of
      the TOGAF® Standard," in *The TOGAF® Standard,
      10th Edition, Introduction and Core Concepts*,
      's-Hertogenbosch: Van Haren Publishing, 2022.

[8]   Business Architecture Guild®. *A Guide to the Business
      Architecture Body of Knowledge*®, vol. 11.0. 2022.

[9]   Ziemann, Jörg. *Fundamentals of Enterprise
      Architecture Management*. Cham: Springer
      Nature, 2022.

[10] Maier, Mark, Emery, David, and Hilliard, Rich.
      "Software architecture: introducing IEEE
      Standard 1471," https://ieeexplore.ieee.org/
      document/917550, 2001.

[11] Wierda, Gerben. *Mastering ArchiMate Edition III.
      TC1*. Heerlen: R&A, 2017.

[12] The Open Group, *ArchiMate® 3.2 Specification*.
      's-Hertogenbosch: Van Haren Publishing, 2023.

[13] Gartner. "Gartner Magic Quadrant for Enterprise
      Architecture Tools." www.gartner.com/en/
      documents/4022077, 2022.

[14] Object Management Group. "Business Process
      Model and Notation (BPMN)." www.omg.org/
      spec/BPMN.

[15]   The Open Group. *The TOGAF® Standard, 10th Edition, ADM Practitioner's Guide.* 's-Hertogenbosch: Van Haren Publishing, 2022.

[16]   The Open Group. "What is an EA Capability and EA," in *The TOGAF® Standard, 10th Edition, Leader's Guide,* 's-Hertogenbosch: Van Haren Publishing, 2022.

[17]   The Open Group. *The TOGAF® Standard, 10th Edition, Architecture Development Method.* 's-Hertogenbosch: Van Haren Publishing, 2022.

[18]   The Open Group. "Applying the Organization Map," in *The TOGAF® Standard, 10th Edition, Architecture Development Method,* 's-Hertogenbosch: Van Haren Publishing, 2022.

[19]   Business Architecture Guild®. "Information Mapping," in *A Guide to the Business Architecture Body of Knowledge®,* 2022.

[20]   The Open Group. "Information Mapping," in *The TOGAF® Standard, 10th Edition, Business Architecture,* 's-Hertogenbosch: Van Haren Publishing, 2022.

[21]   The Open Group. "Stakeholder Management," in *The TOGAF® Standard, 10th Edition, Architecture Development Method,* 's-Hertogenbosch: Van Haren Publishing, 2022.

[22]   The Open Group. *The TOGAF® Standard, 10th Edition, Content, Capability, and Governance.* 's-Hertogenbosch: Van Haren Publishing, 2022.

REFERENCES

[23]   ISACA. "Capability Maturity Model Integration (CMMI)," https://cmmiinstitute.com/cmmi/intro.

[24]   National Association of State Chief Information Officers. "NASCIO EA Maturity Model," www.nascio.org/wp-content/uploads/2019/11/NASCIO-EAMM.pdf, vol. 1.3. National Association of State Chief Information Officers, Lexington, KY, 2003.

[25]   van den Berg, Martin, and van Steenbergen, Marlies. *Building an Enterprise Architecture Practice*. Dordrecht: Springer, 2006.

[26]   The Open Group. "Architecture Principles," in *The TOGAF® Standard, 10th Edition, Architecture Development Method*, 's-Hertogenbosch: Van Haren Publishing, 2022.

[27]   Harvard Business School Online. "5 keys to successful strategy execution," https://online.hbs.edu/blog/post/strategy-execution, 2020.

[28]   Doran, George. "There's a S.M.A.R.T. way to write management's goals and objectives." https://community.mis.temple.edu/mis0855002fall2015/files/2015/10/S.M.A.R.T-Way-Management-Review.pdf, 1981.

[29]   Business Architecture Guild®. "Initiative Mapping," in *A Guide to the Business Architecture Body of Knowledge®*, 2022.

[30]   Kuehn, Whynde. *Strategy to Reality*. New York: Morgan James Publishing, 2023.

Index

Printed in the United States
by Baker & Taylor Publisher Services